Tales
from
Annapolis

(A Ring-Knockers' Bedtime Companion)

Compiled by

Rich Zino, Class of '67
Paul Laric, Class of '49

Omega Resources

Published by Omega Resources
249 Hamilton Road
Rockville Centre, NY 11570

ISBN 0-9704710-0-9

Cover Design by Charles Cutler
900 East Meadow Avenue
North Bellmore, NY 11710

Printed in the United States of America

Why This Book?

Remember the sovereign rule:
don't say it; write it.
Of the ten million great stories
that have been told to admiring friends,
especially by Irishmen in their pubs
(and, no doubt, when shipmates get
together),
literature consists of 5000 that were written
down.
If it's not written, it doesn't exist.

James A. Michener

Foreword

The U. S. Naval Academy at Annapolis has a strong tradition of developing graduates with singular qualities of leadership, integrity, honor and dedication to service of country. What makes the four-year experience at Annapolis unique is the diverse, demanding curriculum of academics and intense professional training, serendipitously mixed with a heavy dose of "character-building" opportunities.

And just what is "character-building?" Well, that's the subject of this book, as told through the experiences of graduates from the Class of 1931 through the Class of 1994.

So sit back and relax. Pull out your favorite pipe, put your feet up on the nearest table and take a look at these tales of uncommon Annapolis phenomena.

The Laws

"Now these are the Laws of the Navy, unwritten and varied they be..."

From the days of Plebe Summer *The Laws of the Navy* were viewed as just another rate to memorize and regurgitate on command. None of us doubted the wisdom of *The Laws*. Although they were based on values handed down from the days of "wooden ships and iron men," the precepts are as valid today as they were back then.

Ronald Arthur Hopwood, 1868-1949, was a Rear Admiral in the British Royal Navy, a poet and writer, especially on naval gunnery. Best known for his *Laws of the Navy*, he also wrote *Secret Orders*, according to *The New Century Handbook of English Literature.*

Those of us far removed from Plebe year – many of us now retired – may look on *The Laws* more kindly than we did as Plebes while "shoved out" in an upper classman's room. You may even decide that you want to memorize a verse or two all over again.

For this, and for a bit of nostalgia, we purloined *The Laws* to use as a point of departure for each of our 27 chapters in an attempt to categorize the stories and anecdotes that follow (although some would argue that they defy any attempt at organization).

By what right have we done this? Well, *The Laws* taught us to take advantage of all available resources to accomplish the task at hand. We did just that.

The Editors.

Acknowledgments

The editors acknowledge with gratitude the permission given by the publishers of *Naval Institute Proceedings* to reprint several articles appearing in past issues of their publication.

A special thanks goes to Bob Hunt '67 who provided the 27 illustrations of *The Laws* and who helped us with a timely sanity check when our progress seemed dead in the water.

And it is with deepest gratitude that we say thank you to all of the alumni who sent in personal stories and anecdotes about their days at the U.S.Naval Academy. Some are amusing, others are poignant, but all of them bring back many memories of our own days as Midshipmen and, together, they provide insights into the experiences we all shared.

Whether the readers be fellow alumni, or are just curious about what makes Annapolis grads tick, we hope they will derive as much enjoyment from these tales as we did in compiling them.

Table Of Contents

The Laws of the Navy

I

Now these are the Laws of the Navy

Unwritten and varied they be;

And he that is wise will observe them,

Going down in his ship to the sea.

Excerpts from Presidents Carter's Speech in the Naval Academy Chapel, June 4th, 1996

When we came in and sat down, I noticed that Rosalynn was laughing almost aloud. I said, "Rosalynn, you have forgotten that this is a memorial service. Everything is supposed to be very solemn." She showed me the bottom line on the program, and it said, "Congregation, if able, standing." That is one indication that it's different times, but I share with Bill Crowe the excitement and pleasure at looking out at an audience of so many of the members of the Class of '47.

She and I were out last night about nine-thirty, and we decided to walk around the grounds and look at the old buildings that we knew when I was here with you. Memories flooded back. A lot of the buildings are new since then, of course. Some memories are very solemn, some frivolous. I couldn't get out of my mind singing the song which some of you may remember, "Fearless Fosdick Is Our Guide." Do you remember that? We share a lot of things in common, but we had different motivations in wanting to come to Annapolis for our education and an opportunity to shape our lives.

When I was five years old in the little town of Plains, Georgia, where we still live, if anyone asked me what I wanted to do when I grew up I didn't say I wanted to be a cowboy or a fireman. I said, like a parrot, that I wanted to go to Annapolis. It was a life-time ambition of mine. My father was a second lieutenant in the Army in the First World War, but I had an uncle – my mother's youngest brother – who was my Navy hero. His name was Tom Gordy.

Tom Gordy was a radioman second-class on Guam and was captured two weeks or so after Pearl Harbor. He was taken to Japan.

He had a wife and three kids who lived with us in Georgia. After two years we were all notified that Tom was dead. His wife, Dorothy, was from San Francisco, and she moved back home. A year later, she married a family friend. When the war was over, they found Tom alive. He weighed less than a hundred pounds. He had been working on a twelve-mile long railroad, hauling coal out of the Japanese mountains down to a shipping point. They made him a full Lieutenant when he was found and gave him back pay for four years. Uncle Tom had a great sense of humor. He was a light-weight boxing champion of the Pacific Fleet. He had a great ability to tease me. I always said the Navy made a serious mistake when they promoted him from radioman second class to be a Senior Lieutenant. He said that the country would make a much greater mistake if they promoted a Lieutenant Senior grade to be Commander in Chief. But of course, in 1976, they did that. Tom and I were good friends. By the way, I wrote a poem about Tom Gordy in a book of poetry called "Always a Reckoning"…which Rosalynn asked me to announce is still on sale.

I think all of us began to shape or solidify our lives' priorities when we were here. Red Hertzog and others who were with me then have often reminded each other of Plebe year. I was a Georgian, a southerner who absolutely refused to sing "*Marching Through Georgia*." And as I look around this crowd, I don't think there was anyone who got more licks with a bread pan, a big spoon at serving time or a broom at night. I don't think anyone has ever run the commando course before reveille more than I did. And I

11

have always been grateful for that because that experience in Plebe year prepared me for later life in politics.

Another thing that shaped our lives, in addition to Plebe year, was our experience with commanding officers. When we were graduated, as you remember, we had to be on surface ships or their equivalent for two years. Then we were able to go into the Air Force or Submarines to Naval Intelligence or whatever. I put in for submarines.

I had a series of commanding officers who really shaped the basic principles by which I've lived. Some did not demonstrate the high standards of professionalism that I had anticipated when I was graduated form this institution. Other, I would say, equaled or exceeded the standards that we expected. I think my best skipper was a man named J.B.Williams, Jr., who was skipper of the first submarine on which I served, *USS Pomfret* (SS-391). He was a man of stern discipline; we all knew exactly where we stood, but he never had to chastise us. He was a man of gentleness. He shared with us our problems and our ideals; our fears; our concerns; our hopes and dreams. We tried never to fail him, not because we feared punishment but because we didn't want to let our skipper down. That made a great impact on my life.

Later, I served under Admiral Hyman Rickover. Many of you have had the same exhilarating experience. I served under Rickover in the earliest stages of the nuclear program. Classmate Chuck Carlisle and I were together in Schenectady, NY preparing the second atomic submarine, *Seawolf*. I served under Rickover before he mellowed. I hear laughter going through the group. He mellowed with me after I was elected President and he and I became great friends then, but I feared him, I respected him, and I thank that as much as my own father, Rickover helped shape my life. Between J.B.Williams, Jr., a gentle but firm commanding officer, and Admiral Rickover, an always stern and demanding leader, I was heavily influenced. I know all of you were shaped and influenced by your own skippers. I try to be, in my own leadership capacity, now and before, more like J.B.Williams, Jr., but many of my subordinates say that I am more like Rickover. I heard one of them the other day say that "When we make plans for the future, we look at the calendar, but Jimmy looks at his watch."

Well, those background thoughts of pre-Academy days, days here for three years, experiences in the Navy after we left bind us all together in highly different ways. No two of us are alike, but I think that the basic ideals of life, the moral values by which we live, have been shaped by the Navy. I know mine have. I've been distressed the last few months, I'll say, by some of the so-called Navy scandals. I was asked outside the Chapel by a television crew, "What about the Navy scandals?" and I point out to them that this was a transient problem. I quoted my high school teacher Miss Julia Colman – I also quoted her during my inaugural address – who said, "We all must accommodate changing times, but cling to unchanging values." To me, that's what the Navy does.

I was a southerner from the deep south. Almost all my playmates were African-American boys. We worked in the same fields, we fished in the same creeks, we plowed with the same mule, we played on the same baseball team. But there was a rigid life of segregation in my community, and indeed, all over the Nation because the U.S.Supreme Court ruled, I think erroneously, that "separate but equal" was justified as a way of life under the Constitution of our Nation. It was here at the Naval Academy that the Class of 1947 first faced that challenge when a young Midshipman, two years behind us, Wesley Brown, came to the Naval Academy, the first African-American midshipman. We reacted in different ways. It was not easy for me, as a southerner to accept the standard of equality. He and I were both on the cross-country team. There we were judged by performance. Wesley Brown always came in first. I generally came in near the last. But here, and later in my submarine life, I saw the Navy face a difficult challenge of societal change and the Navy prevailed.

I have always been grateful to President Truman, who was our Commander-in-Chief, when he mandated long before the civil rights laws were passed that there should be racial equality on ships of the United States Navy. I don't remember a single dissenting voice on the submarine in which I served, when we were required to treat African-American sailors with total equality.

There the Navy was on the cutting edge of change, clinging to values that never change. Our Nation is now going through the process of learning how to treat women with the respect they deserve. The "Tailhook" scandals have been embarrassing to me but they have been helpful, I believe, in dramatizing and demonstrating to the Nation that all of us need to improve our attitudes. I deplore the bad publicity, but I have an innate sense of appreciation...an innate sense of confidence...an innate sense of certainty that our high navy values have not and never will change.

I am very proud of the members of the Class of '47. I am particularly proud of the two members who won the Congressional Medal of Honor. America is a land of courage, but this recognition of the willingness...even, I would say, eagerness....under pressure voluntarily to offer one's own life...with that expectation...for the lives or life of a shipmate is indeed something that all of us should find to be sobering. And I want to pay special tribute this morning to those two of our Classmates who won the Medal of Honor.

We all want to be leading lives of significance. I am not going to go down the long list of those who are no longer with us, but just as an example I would like to mention my three roommates who fall in the roles of those who are deceased. One was James Andrews, from a little town in Iowa. He was my roommate as a Plebe. He had a degree in engineering from Iowa State University before he came here. He was a serious student but one always willing to share what he knew with those of us who were struggling for the first time with some of the challenges of the academic year. Another roommate of mine who is no longer with us was Blu Middleton, red-haired, full of life, always wanted to be a U.S.Marine, which he was, from Deer Lodge, Montana. Another one was Robert Scott from Phoenix, Arizona. He was the champion classical pianist of his state. Quite often, Midshipmen would gather around him as he played the piano. I was lucky to be his roommate. He introduced me to classical music and out of our four dollars a month or seven dollars a month, we would immediatcly go the the record store, and we would buy different versions of all four of Rachmaninoff's concertos and compare the techniques with Bob being my teacher how those concertos were played; Rachmaninoff, Rubenstein and others. We had one recording of Tristan and Isolde and it was very interesting because at the start of the final movement, "Liebestod," Bob Scott would always turn up the volume on our record player and open the door. In Bancroft Hall there would generally be about fifteen or twenty Midshipmen standing around listening to that

15

recording before it was over. Bob Scott is no longer with us either.

There are about two hundred others about whom every one of you would have the same kind of vivid appreciation...I think it is good, in closing my remarks, to point out that they leave a great heritage...all those who passed away from combat or from other causes. They have a heritage of families – I think one of our Classmates has 53 grand-children...I am very envious...Rosalynn and I have nine – of friends...like those assembled here today, and as I have already mentioned earlier, a heritage of freedom, because each one of them, as we remember them, has contributed to that cause.

I brought out my old dog-eared copy of the *Bluejackets Manual* that they issued the first day we were here, and I read the code described in this little book...not just for officers, not just for Midshipmen, but for every person who serves in the Navy...and I jotted down these words that I would like to read in closing;

"Those who serve in ships are expected to exhibit" ...listen to these words and remember your Classmates who have fallen..."are expected to exhibit, obedience, knowledge, fighting spirit, reliability, loyalty, initiative, self-control, energy, courage, justice, faith in ourselves, cheerfulness and honor, but above all" the *Bluejackets Manual* says, "comes absolute truth," and I am quoting again, "the final test of a man." These are sobering words, not sad words, but unchanging words and inspirational words, and, I think, words appropriate for the memory of the two hundred members of our Class of '47 who are no longer with us.

Jimmy Carter '47

Marching Extra Duty

It was Plebe Summer in 1980. Naturally it was a sweltering weekend day in Annapolis that summer. I was marching extra duty with my roommate Bryan Stolley. To add insult to injury, it was Brian's 18th birthday. I can't recall what infraction placed us amongst the lucky group of Plebes that day, but I am sure that if I could remember what it was it would only bring a smile and laugh today.

We were marching the extra duty and dutifully sweating bullets as the mid-day sun beat down upon us. The tourists were out and about the yard, and there we were, hot, miserable and marching extra duty.

In the middle of our "tour" the first class Midshipman who was in charge of our detail brought us to a halt at a far corner of Dewey Field, out of ear shot of the tourists. He then proceeded to tell us that we should be proud of our achievement of gaining admission to the Naval Academy. He spoke about how we were the best and brightest that the country had to offer. He further mentioned that the tourists had no idea why we were marching and that we should give them the best show possible.

At that point we resumed marching with everyone's head held high. Despite the heat and exhaustion of the moment, the leadership shown to us by this first classman made everyone proud and motivated on an occasion that was one of the most miserable, both physically and mentally, that most of us had ever had to endure in our lives. After weeks of a hot and arduous Plebe Summer, he had the leadership skills to motivate us even under those circumstances.I knew instantly that I had made the right decision when I chose to attend the Naval Academy. In my mind, this example of leadership exemplified all that Annapolis stands for.

Eric Rosen '84

The Path to Annapolis

The path taken to the Naval Academy by the thousands who have arrived there involve, I am sure, events that are simple, complex, planned, accidental and just about any reason one can imagine. Additionally, I am sure more than a few feelings of uncertainty occurred in most of them. In my own case arriving at the Academy and staying there, involved a couple of very fortunate occurrences.

My own path to the Academy started while cutting the grass! Our Congressman lived in my neighborhood and I would occasionally cut his lawn. In small mid-western towns during the late 40's, cutting grass and delivering papers were common ways to make a little money. I would visit with him from time to time when he was home. One day he came out of his house and said to me, "Have you ever thought about going to one of the Service Academies?" I said no, though thought to myself the idea was more interesting than cutting lawns. I told him it sounded interesting although at that point in time I had never met a Naval Officer. He was one of the Congressmen who gave his own exam to help in selecting his candidates. I took the exam and ended up as his principal appointment to Annapolis that year. When I got in the train to go to the Academy, I had never in my life been east of Gary, Indiana.

Needless to say, during the early months, there were many bouts of homesickness and an occasional thought of calling my family and telling them I was coming home. That all changed one afternoon when I was out for a walk in the Yard. Walking towards me on the same path was the President of the United States, Harry Truman, chatting with a senior Naval Officer. No Secret Service agents, no limos, just the two of them – this was years ago.

As our paths met he broke into a big grin and put out his hand. "How are you, young man?" I said I was fine (I lied). He asked who appointed me to the Academy and I said Noah Mason of Illinois. Truman said, "I have known Noah for years. He is a fine man." We chatted for a few minutes and as he started to walk away he said, "I am glad you are here. This is a very important place to all of us."

I never forgot that comment. It caused me to recognize the importance of what I was doing. It was a turning point and I never looked back. Were I to go through life again, I wouldn't change a thing.

James R. Hocking '53

First Impressions

When I entered the Academy in July of 1943 on what was literally the last day for admission to the Class of 1947, I was assigned as the third man in what would, during the academic year, be a two-man room. I had completed two years of engineering at Purdue and was in the V5 aviation cadet program when offered the appointment.

Being loaded down with all my newly issued gear on a blistering hot day, my knock on the door was answered by a blond, stocky Midshipman who said "Hi, my name's Nimitz, what's yours?" I merely replied "Hemmer." He then said "I'm here on a Presidential, how'd you get in?" At that point I had heard about enough, so I said "I'm here on a Congressional Third Alternate, but I'11 tell you one thing, Junior, I'll be here when you leave!"

Although I had long forgotten that smart remark, Charlie Nimitz hadn't. June week he reminded me of it and said that every time he had any difficulty that could affect his tenure at the Academy, he would remember that I was still there, and bear down. Recounting this incident should not be viewed as evidence of any antagonism between us. Charlie was a fine person in every respect. Periodically Chester, who was his uncle, would drive down from Washington to see how he was getting along. Charlie's father was on duty somewhere in the Pacific. The Admiral would come through the gate without stopping and drive up the ramp in front of Bancroft Hall. Everyone on duty with any sense knew they had better find Charlie right away.

Twice Charlie insisted I go with him to meet his uncle, who dismissed all Aides and asked us both numerous questions about the entire routine and how we were doing.

He assured us he could handle any complaints or criticisms without any repercussions against us. Charlie was used to somewhat more "attention" than I received from the upper classmen, but he never voiced any criticism whatever. Of course, neither did I. I've often thought it would have been interesting to see what happened had Charlie decided to register a complaint.

Edward H. Hemmer '47

II

As naught may outrun the destroyer,

So it is with the law and its grip.

For the strength of the ship is the Service,

And the strength of the Service, the ship.

Nice Shoes

During the final weeks before graduation in 1967, I was driving around the outskirts of Annapolis one humid evening in search of a suitable eating establishment, accompanied by my classmate and good buddy Dick Zino and two lovely ladies. After rejecting several of our favorite haunts because of the crowds, we finally pulled into a restaurant some distance from the Academy but, we felt sure, well within the ten-mile limit which in those days defined the boundary of authorized travel for all Midshipmen.

As it turned out, we were just outside the ten-mile limit. We should have known, if only from the fact that there were no other white-uniformed patrons in sight. Our minds, no doubt, were on other, more important things. Like food, women and the glory of our impending graduation.

And so it was a rude shock when, as we waited our turn to pay the cashier, a mufti-clad man with short hair suddenly approached us.

"Excuse me, are you guys Midshipmen at the Naval Academy?" Had I been asked that question in the mental state of jaded adulthood I currently enjoy, my reaction would certainly have been one of undisguised sarcasm.

"No, actually we're on our way to a nautical theme party. Would you care to join us?"

Instead, Dick and I blurted out "yes sir" in unhesitating unison without the slightest hint of satiric wit.

The inquisitor quickly reached into his pocket, pulled out his wallet, showed us his ID card and proclaimed, "I'm Lieutenant Commander so-and-so and I'd like to know what you're doing outside the ten-mile limit."

"No excuse, sir ... we didn't realize we were outside the ten-mile limit, sir...."

Following a brief skeptical roll of the eyes, he directed us to return immediately to the Academy and report to the Officer of the Watch, adding that he would call ahead and explain the nature of our offense.

Dick and I headed back to the drag house, dropped off our dates who had no clue about what was going on, and promptly reported to Bancroft Hall as ordered. The Officer of the Watch was making his rounds at the time, so the Midshipman Officer of the Watch instructed us to stand by.

"Is it OK if we go downstairs to the bowling alley while we're waiting?"

"Sure," the MOOW replied, "I'11 give you a call when the OOW gets back."

As I look back some thirty years later, it occurs to me that this incident (I'11 share the rest of the story in a moment) represents several unique aspects of the Academy experience. The expectation of perfection from superiors, subordinates and peers, as well as the remarkable willingness of most Midshipmen to obediently strive for and readily accept the pursuit of perfection.

Interwoven with this idyllic quest for perfection, there was the spontaneous cultivation among Midshipmen of a dash-of-humor demeanor, which routinely revealed itself in the face of personal and professional challenges, ranging from the petty to the most serious of matters. A demeanor born of four difficult years of daily saturation m the ideals and realities of what it means to be a subordinate, to be a superior, to be a leader, in a demanding, often unforgiving, profession.

During my subsequent years of military service, I found that Academy graduates, including those from West Point and the Air Force Academy, invariably and unlike most officers I observed, approached their personal and professional lives with an underlying sense of humor which softened yet seldom compromised their pursuit of perfection.

Now back to the Bancroft Hall bowling alley in early summer 1967. As Dick Zino and I awaited the return of the OOW and the call to report to his office, I recollect feeling no underlying sense of humor about much of anything at that particular moment. When the summons finally came, we hurriedly abandoned our bowling balls and scrambled upstairs to meet our fate.

The OOW scolded us as we expected him to do and remarked that he would forward his report to our Company Officer so we could serve the appropriate time on restriction.

While all this was going on, I became aware that I was still wearing my bowling shoes. Perhaps the OOW won't notice. Please don't notice, sir.

When I was finally dismissed and turned to depart, his voice called out.

"Oh, Mr. Hunt...." I did an about face just short of the door and looked into the eyes of a smiling OOW. "Nice shoes!"

Bob Hunt '67

Editor's Note: Ever the iconoclast, Bob spent a career in the Army, mostly as a Chinese specialist in Counter-intelligence. Bob now refuses to work and amuses himself by dabbling in various artistic endeavors such as singing and playing his banjo for strangers, who typically keep a safe distance while remarking, "what an odd fellow."

Nice Shoes, Different Recollection

It was a Saturday evening in early spring of our first class year. Mary Ellen had traveled down from New York to visit and plans were for the two of us to join with Bob Hunt and his date Maggie to go out to dinner in a nice restaurant in Parole Plaza where we understood several of our classmates would be gathering. There was to be an informal get-together later on at a motel out of town where another classmate's drag was staying. As was our practice, Mary Ellen would drive my car that I had secreted away in a garage in town, rented from Mr. Economy, an elderly Greek who, at the end of a weekend when I returned my car to his garage, frequently invited me in to his kitchen for a glass of schnapps. Well, Mary Ellen drove my car, an old 1960 four-door Ford Falcon, with a Syracuse University decal on the back window and a Fort Belvoir parking sticker on the bumper (to disguise it as something other than a Midshipman vehicle) and picked us up by Gate 3.

We hopped in the car, me in the passenger seat, Bob and Maggie in the back, and headed for Parole Plaza. But because we were running late, by the time we arrived, there was easily an hour wait for a table. Midshipmen lives are planned to the split second and none of us has the patience to waste an hour, even for a good dinner. So we decided to catch a meal elsewhere and we drove out Route 50 to look for an appropriate alternative. Before long we spotted a Howard Johnson's near an exit, parked the car and went inside, encountering no waiting line. The meal was quite adequate and the price was right. Little did we suspect that we had happened beyond the ten-mile limit (from the Chapel

Dome) in violation of our liberty regulations. When we went to the cashier to pay we were accosted by a Lieutenant Commander who informed us that we were "on report." He took our names and instructed us to return immediately to Bancroft Hall and said that he was placing a call to the Officer of the Day. Being proper Midshipmen, we answered "Aye, aye, sir!" and proceeded to follow his orders.

It was dark out and, as we exited the parking lot, Mary Ellen turned right onto the divided highway, headed away from the Academy, not realizing that a left turn across a break in the median was possible. We immediately knew we were in double trouble. As soon as possible we hung a "Uey," reversing our course, but since we were expected at that motel party, which was nearby, we decided to stop in and advise our friends that we wouldn't be joining them. No sooner did we park and get out of the car but we heard police sirens heading our way. "Shoot! They're after us," we thought. We ran into the motel room, like common criminals and hid behind the curtains, convinced that an all-points bulletin had been put out for us.

As it turned out, the police had responded to a 911 call resulting from a guest having a heart attack in another motel room. We were shaking like two leafs in a storm. The evening was ruined, we'd likely spend the rest of the weekend restricted to our rooms, not to mention mucho demerits to be worked off over succeeding weekends.

We didn't linger in the motel room, but headed straight back to the yard. All the way back our lives flashed before our eyes. This was it. Our careers were ruined. How could we explain our stupidity to the Officer of the Day? Or was that officer back at Howard Johnson's just bluffing? Maybe he didn't telephone back to the Academy. Maybe we could skate out on this infraction. But, discretion being the better part of valor, we returned to Bancroft Hall in short order. We headed to my room and, lo and behold, waiting on my desk was a chit from the duty officer ordering me to report to him ASAP.

Next stop: Bob's room and, sure enough, there was an identical chit on his desk. We straightened our ties, buffed the toes of our shoes on the back of the opposite pant legs, and off we went to face the music.

Bob was a three-striper and had a lot more to lose than I. I not only felt awful for my own predicament, but I felt responsible for getting him in trouble. The OOD that night was a Marine Corps Major with a reputation for being a hard ass. Why did this have to happen on his watch? After a lengthy wait, we were ushered into his office and he proceeded to lambaste us, up one side and down the other. It was bad enough being beyond the ten-mile limit, but to be in uniform...we were practically begging to be put on report. Then, after being told to return directly to Bancroft Hall, the reporting officer observed us defying his order as we turned away from the Academy heading for Washington, D.C. The Major said he could drum us out of the Academy for pulling this stunt. But he claimed that no one could actually be as stupid as we appeared to be, so he was giving us the benefit of the doubt. Bob would keep his stripes, and we would receive only 75 demerits each, which meant restriction to Bancroft Hall for the next several weekends. We responded "Aye, aye, sir!," saluted, did a sharp "about face" and left his office.

Believe it or not, it all turned out better than we had expected. First, we could have been "Class A'd" and considered for expulsion...but weren't; second, the brass never found out the I had been illegally keeping a car hidden in town, surely grounds for dismissal; third, the weekends of restriction gave us no excuse not to study for some important upcoming exams; and lastly, 30 years later this incident remains one of the most vivid recollections of my days at the Academy.

By the way, I married Mary Ellen and, to this day she's stood by my side during good times and bad. Compared with the highs and lows we experienced that Saturday night many years ago, our life together has been a breeze.

Looking back on those Midshipman days makes one wonder, where else besides one of the service academies would a 22 year old college student live in fear of being a mile beyond an arbitrary radius of a school landmark? Where else would being in uniform work to aggravate an otherwise minor infraction? Where else would a Lieutenant Commander relish the sadistic delight of intentionally destroying the weekend, and blemishing the otherwise clean service performance records for two Midshipmen, without trying to ascertain the facts surrounding the incident, and further imply that those Midshipmen had flagrantly disobeyed his direct orders? I pity the officers and enlisted men that had the misfortune to serve under him. There are few people who, 30 years later, I would thoroughly enjoy punching out, but this Lieutenant Commander is one of them.

Richard Zino '67

Restricted Again

Restriction to Bancroft hall was commonplace. Few midshipmen have been able to avoid the occasional infractions that bring demerits and some form of weekend restriction. Those who are so punished are required to muster for inspection several times each day in Smoke Hall behind the Rotunda to bear evidence of their presence while their fellow midshipmen are enjoying liberty.

Back in the late 1980's, this was certainly the case, and many midshipmen at the time will remember a very attractive, very well-proportioned female company officer. During one of these musters a young restrictee was standing at attention, but couldn't avoid becoming sexually aroused by the proximity of the blond and buxom Marine Corps captain. It didn't require a particularly close inspection for her to notice his "gear adrift," and she asked him about it, wanting to know what it was, exactly, that was out of place.

He gulped as she poked it for emphasis and, finally, sweating profusely, admitted "It's…mmm…me….Ma'am."

Tom Williams '88

30

A Night on the Town

"Hey, you up for some Chinese?" the voice drawled from the direction of my front door. I looked up from my book to see the small frame of my company and classmate, Al Slawson, in the passageway.

"No, not tonight, Al. I'm not hungry. Just gonna relax," I replied, looking back down at the page.

"What do you mean?" the fiery Georgian replied, entering the room. "I've got Amy down here for the Ring Dance. That only comes once in a lifetime. Most everyone's out tonight, and we sure don't want to go alone. You're it."

"Thanks, but no, " I said, briefly glancing up now.

"The heck with you then," I heard him say as he turned to leave. Al certainly had a persuasive method that merited psychological scrutiny; I felt like a bilger for wanting to complete reading my novel.

"Okay, give me just a second", I recanted, getting up to tuck my shirt back into my summer white trousers.

"Great," he beamed, "Amy and I will be in the Rotunda waiting," and with that, he disappeared.

I followed shortly, greeting the couple one deck below my 4-2 room. We headed out through T-Court towards the Chapel, as it was decided we were going to the New Canton, one of two Chinese restaurants in all of Annapolis at the time, I believe. Passing the Chapel we cut across the grass, making a beeline for Gate 3 and Maryland Avenue. The Yard was unusually abandoned this evening, which may have contributed to my not heeding the sawhorses, around which Amy and Al gave wide berth.

A teeth-jarring jolt was the next instant I realized in the darkness, as my left leg disappeared into the ground up to the knee. Shock turned to embarrassment, as I realized I had fallen into a plumbing dig in the middle of the small field. It was a good thing no one else was around; my two friends suppressed laughter through grins.

"Gee, Hoov, I guess you'd better go back and change," Al finally came up with the quick solution.

"Yeah, I guess so. You can wait for me?"

"Sure, we'll be here. Some June Week for you, huh?" It didn't occur to me that Al may have been thinking I had done this on purpose due to my previous reluctance, because I was too busy trying to elude any officers of the watch on my way back to the Hall. Demerits during June Week would have been a "real bummer. " Fortunately, I was able to avoid any detection by using the 4th Wing second-class door and ladder, thus avoiding notice from anyone in the high-profile Rotunda of Bancroft Hall and its Tecumseh Court approach, all lit up in their splendor.

I reached my room and turned on the overhead lights. My appearance was worse than I had feared. A mixture of red clay and water had dyed my lower left leg a pale red and splattered both the right and upper left leg of my once pure-white trousers. Not to mention the condition of my shoes which were not corfam and would need polishing, and the edges were caked with clay within all of their grooves.

"Please let me have another summer whites! Please tell me I have another summer whites! " I repeated to myself as I headed to my locker. I was in luck for there was a replacement. This attention to detail in being prepared for any eventuality made me almost start to feel like a squared-away Midshipman again.

A wet cloth scrubbed over my shoes and touches of quick polish in some places improved the leather somewhat before the natural red dye could set in. The laces were rinsed and wrung and the edge dressing could only be applied after I had scrubbed away the grout with an old toothbrush. This entire uniform race (an experience I thought I would never have to endure again) seemed to take only five minutes but was probably actually an hour by the time I arrived back at Gate 3.

Neither of my friends seemed to have minded waiting for me a second time. "My God, what patience these people must have! Either that or they're not all that hungry," was my embarrassing thought, as I sullenly walked with the couple out into town.

Dinner itself is a vague memory. I do remember conversation about New England, as Al had met Amy while he was at NAPS, and I believe they were engaged by this time. Bancroft, company, brigade, and academic gossip passed back and forth, in which, in sarcastic retrospect, I'm sure Amy became very involved. My home state of Florida was another topic, and Amy also introduced the historical account of when Caesar had said, "Veni, vidi, vici," and other moments when like expressions had been used. At this point I was in over my head. I was a "bull" major, yes, but not in history, I'm afraid.

I spent one more year in the Thirtieth Company with Al and my other classmates. His interest in professional boxing and all its history infected me, and I'm an avid boxing fan to this day, as a result. That first-class year I also received some ribbing for the 1977 Ford station wagon I "inherited" from my parents. It was dubbed "The Beastmobile," a name which Al helped to perpetuate. At any rate, transportation was transportation, and I was glad to have it, regardless.

Commissioning came too quickly, and, as the old song goes, we scattered far and wide. I remember Al was headed to the frigate *U.S.S. Capodanno*, to which he was very proud to have gotten an assignment. After a couple of years, I had lost contact with all of my company mates as other matters took priority for us all. It was not until a few years later that I got one of the routine phone calls from my parents; they were still receiving my issues of *Shipmate* at their address, and my mother worked into the conversation that she had some news for me. One of my friends had died, and, after bracing me for the worst, she finally told me it was Al Slawson. I was in shock, not only because the man had always seemed so alive to me, but that his death came not in combat or in a flying mishap, situations for which Annapolis prepares us, but rather from an automobile accident with a drunken driver.

I had to see the "Last Call" section to eliminate my disbelief. On receiving a copy, I read that Al had actually left the Navy a few months earlier, and he and Amy had an infant son. My next thought was about poor Amy, for those two had been inseparable. Unfortunately, grief works both ways, and I did not get up the nerve to send my condolences until a couple of years later, as my thoughts continued to go back to my days at the Academy. I had been going through my old uniforms and found a light, but large, red stain on the back of one of my summer white trousers. Somehow, this pair ended up remaining in my closet, while the others went for sale at the local Army-Navy Surplus.

I received a reply from her about a month later. It seemed all was forgiven from her extremely upbeat letter. She commented on my daughter's photo that I had sent and admitted she was now working as a hospital pharmacist; this nearly floored me for I was working as a clinical pharmacist for a home infusion company. Perhaps we both had the same uncanny insight to the job market.

The most compelling, however, was she felt now that her son, Clayton, was the "entire world" to her; I believed this to be an appropriate, but nevertheless, strong-willed statement.

Next was the recent photo of Clayton: it was of a boy with a smiling face, bespectacled like his father. Yet, readiness to take on all of the world's challenges, like his dad did, could be read on his countenance. Al may have been gone, but his spirit remained behind. However, I still like to imagine him in heaven convincing fellow alumni to go out for a night on the town.

David Hoover '84

III

Take heed what ye say of your seniors,

Be your words spoken softly or plain,

Lest a bird of the air tell the matter

And so ye shall hear it again.

Who Gets the Brick?

One of the most enduring traditions at the U.S.Naval Academy is also one of the most mysterious and, for some, the most feared. While many of the other character-building activities are targeted at the Plebe class, this one is aimed primarily at first and second classmen and is carried out by the Plebes. It's called the "bricking ceremony" and it occurs almost every weekend during the academic year in a few, or sometimes in many, company areas throughout Bancroft Hall simultaneously.

Description of the "Ceremony":
"It would normally start on a Sunday night about 8:00 p.m. A Plebe would be summoned into a first class Midshipman's room and be directed to form a "bricking party." The Plebe would ask eight or ten of his classmates to meet in his room, from which they would then venture, typically all in b-robes, carrying a brick mounted on a pillow, chanting, "Who gets the brick? Who gets the brick?" As this group meandered about the company area of Bancroft Hall, all of the other Plebes and various upperclassmen would join the mass, and the volume of the dreaded chant would increase. Finally, after building up as much suspense as possible, the assembled group would stop in front of a room (typically, a first classman). The Plebe in charge would enter the room, sound off (announcing his name) and proclaim his purpose was to present the brick to the targeted Midshipman, Mr. X.

If Mr. X were a good sport, he would graciously accept the brick and allow himself to be thrown into his shower, clothes and all, and the ceremony would soon be over. On the other hand, if he were not of such a mind, he would refuse to accept the brick, thereby challenging the group to present it to him, and a virtual free-for-all would ensue, whereby he would take as many Plebes into the shower with him as he could. In the end, however, he would have been presented with the brick - the only question was the manner in which he would accept it.

Actual Uses:

The purpose of the bricking ceremony was to recognize that upperclassman who had been seen with the ugliest "drag," whether a "blind date" or of his own invitation, over that weekend.

In the high-testosterone, unisex environment of the '60s Naval Academy, many of us felt that we were God's gift to the human race, or at least the female half thereof. Virtually all had seen themselves as high-profile "studs" during their high school careers, filling leadership positions and excelling in academics and varsity athletics. Many of us perceived that the beauty and sex appeal of our dates was somehow a valid reflection of ourselves. Conversely, one who could not attract a centerfold-quality date was somehow perceived as being deficient; and, by extrapolation, the loser in this "contest" would receive the dreaded brick "award."

Actual Misuses:

The "Who gets the brick?" ceremony was also subject to various misuses (as if the fundamental purpose, when viewed through 30+ years of hindsight, was not a misuse). For example, when one announced an engagement to be married to the drag he had escorted that weekend; it was common for that Midshipman to be presented with the brick - somewhat of a perversely humorous acknowledgment by his peers of the event. Another misuse was the presentation of the brick to support one side of a "power play" between two Midshipmen of the same class. It also presented an opportunity for Plebes to get even with particularly strict upperclassmen, so a "brick ceremony" could easily get out of control and become downright brutal, with numerous cuts and bruises. And, in perhaps the most perverse misapplication, some Mids would actually have contests to see who could be spotted with the ugliest date, and thereby compete for the "award."

Impacts:

In hindsight, I feel very guilty to have participated so enthusiastically in these puerile activities. I can recall the pain and suffering we inadvertently caused when bricking the mid who was dragging one whom he considered his "grease girl," e.g., one he had secretly become engaged to or would even seriously consider marrying. Obviously, one can draw conclusions regarding the impact the above mindset had regarding our attitudes towards women (one might properly argue that such could contribute to the mentality that became known with the "Tailhook scandal" of the '80s). And, the concentration on the physical attributes of women rather than the whole person probably retarded the rate at which we matured. These attitudes leading to denigration of women are especially embarrassing to those of us who have been blessed with wives and daughters.

Robert J. Armstrong '67

The Window

I am Charles N. Calvano (Chuck), '63. I was a member of the "Terrible Tenth" for Plebe and Youngster years. During that time frame there were significant differences between companies in the nature and severity of the Plebe year they gave, and it was universally agreed that 10th company was the toughest. It was largely to address and reduce these differences that the practice of rotating class/company groups among companies was begun with our class. My class/company mates and I spent our last two years in 8th company. I think the company rotation policy has remained in place for most of the intervening years and has, I trust, resulted in more uniform company "cultures."

As part of the 10th company culture of the time, it was almost unheard of for a firstie to "spoon" a Plebe before graduation. And, in fact, except for my own firstie I was not spooned by anyone else in the class of '60 in my company until June Week.

I write the above not to boast that "I had a tougher Plebe year than you" or any such thing, but only to set the context. Otherwise, it might be hard for a grad from a different era to understand that such things as I mention could occur in June Week (which I know is now in May and called Commissioning Week.)

But the above is not part of the "story." Here's my story:

During Plebe year I lived across the hall from a two-man 1st Class ('60) room. One of the occupants (let's call him "Joe") was particularly vigorous in challenging Plebes and, because we lived so close by, my roommates and I got more than our share of his attention. During June Week 1960, a couple of days before "Joe's" graduation, he was preparing his room for a visit by his parents and his girlfriend (a scheduled June Week activity). He decided he wanted to wash the outside of the windows. To do this he intended to sit on the windowsill, with his upper body outside the window, and his feet inside the room.

We lived on the 3rd deck of the 5th wing of Bancroft Hall. On that deck, the windows come to only a few inches above the deck. Remember that Bancroft Hall had a "zero deck" and in this part of Bancroft, the basement was actually above ground. So "Joe's" window was the equivalent of five stories above a concrete loading dock apron. "Joe" soon realized that, in order to reach the upper windows he would have to stretch beyond the point of balance and would fall, unless someone was inside the room holding him. Because June Week activities were in full swing, Bancroft Hall was nearly deserted, but for some reason, I happened to be alone in my room at the time, having gone there to get something. "Joe" came into my room, braced me up and ordered me across the hall to his room. He told me he wanted to wash the outsides of his windows. He told me to sit on the deck, with my feet against the windowsill and to grasp his feet under my armpits and hold him while he reached out as far as he could to clean the glass.

Now, "Joe" had harassed my roommates and me far beyond the norm of even a Tenth Company Plebe year of that time. He frequently took the last of our "gedunk" and was not above helping himself to a handful of homemade cookies from one of our care packages (the unwritten rule of the time was that an upperclassman would never take more than one of something). He had borrowed uniform trousers and returned them with paint on them; he had required thousands of pushups from us and had us "shove out" for hours over the past nine months. While we had often received similar treatment from his classmates, there was usually some reason for it that even we could see.

"Joe" seemed to do it because he just liked it. In general, I had no love, or even respect for "Joe."

So I now found myself in a deserted Bancroft Hall, holding "Joe's" feet under my arms with him totally dependent on me for support as he hung out over a concrete driveway five stories down. I was acutely aware that I had only to raise my arms to have "Joe" permanently out of my life (and everyone else's) - and I certainly would have thought it a fair trade for the way he had treated me and my classmates. I actually ran the consequences through my mind. "The investigators will find my fingerprints; but I've been in this room hundreds of times, doing pushups, folding his laundry for him, etc. They'll never know I was holding him. All I have to do is raise my arms". I wrestled with this moral dilemma for a long five or ten minutes. I only had to raise my arms and let go.

Well, I didn't. I think that took a good deal of character. Despite "Joe's" treatment which I honestly felt (and still do) was way beyond any limit of training or indoctrination; treatment which was degrading and sadistic; treatment which caused me to believe "Joe" was deserving only of my scorn; I could not betray the trust he had put in me on this occasion.

I think there was a character building lesson there. I certainly had other opportunities to honor the trust placed in me by a senior I didn't particularly like or respect. And I believe it was the right thing to do. "Joe" gave me the first opportunity to practice that.

I've never seen "Joe" since his graduation. I understand he retired as an 0-6 and had a distinguished and successful career. I wonder if he remembers the time I could have ended it all. I still sometimes wonder if I did the right thing that day when I held "Joe's" feet (and his life) in my hands. I've sort of convinced myself I did.

Chuck Calvano '63

Night Message

First class year, I lived with Gerry Jacobs (G.K.) in on the 4th deck of the 4th wing overlooking Tecumseh Court. I was station manager of WRNV, and using a "borrowed" album (can you remember vinyl?), we used to wait until just after taps, turn our lights out, and place both speakers in the window.

Playing Eric Burden and the Animals very softly until the line *"We gotta get out of this place"* and then turn the amp up full balls and blast it across Tecumseh Court.

What followed was a lot of catcalls and cheers into the night. We were bullet proof and untraceable, a minor memory of a long time ago.

Don Priest '67

"Private" Line by Enterprising Firsties
Reduces Phone Costs

Never let it be said that Mids aren't entrepreneurial at heart. It was always a travail in the 1950s and '60s to make phone calls from the limited pay telephone rooms set up in Bancroft Hall for Midshipman use (the "Reg Book" proscribed private lines). The old coin rotary dialers would often malfunction and, in those days before cellular (BC), bliss would have been a private phone in one's own room. Add to that the "Dark Ages" and it's easy to see a dauntless trio of 1st Company Firsties getting a "private" line.

Having completed electrical science, electronics, computers, and weapons courses, and having at least two cruises of practical work with internal communications under their belts, these Class of '62 stalwarts undertook a mission to install a line directly into their room with alcove in the 3rd Wing. The challenge was to find a suitable junction box to tap into that would give access to a direct outside line. One was found in the Weapons Department's Luce Hall system and a line was duly run through the tunnels and basement of Mother Bancroft, up Goat Court wall, into the alcove window of the trio's room, and into a gray "confidential" safe, the ever-present upper class "con locker," where the instrument was secreted.

These adventurers enjoyed considerable use of their "private" phone and closely guarded what they had. Unfortunately, toll call records and auditing of Weapons Department calls uncovered the caper and the jig was up. Supposedly, the aggrieving wire was traced back into the "con locker" and the culprits ordered by the Company Officer, one "Stumpy" Sutherland, to stand and deliver.

Others say the Company Officer was inspecting the room, notorious for being unkempt most of the time, and the phone rang inside the "con locker" (a far more interesting ending).

Needless to say, all three earned Black Ns and served out their Class A restrictions without access to a phone! Need proof of this? Just look in the 1962 LUCKY BAG and you'll find one of the perpetrators holding the offending instrument in one hand and the disconnected bitter end in the other.

Robert Black '63

IV

If ye labour from morn until even'

And meet with reproof for your toil,

It is well -- that the guns be humbled,

The compressor must check the recoil.

The Mess Hall (aka King Hall)

We spent a lot of time in the mess hall. Each visit was an occasion not only to draw nutrition from the plentiful and well-balanced meals, but an occasion for the Plebes and upper classmen to interface in a formidable setting.

The tables accommodated ten people each and, typically there would be two first classmen at the head of the table and two second classmen at the foot. Plebes and Youngsters would be arranged on either side with the Plebes in the middle to bear most of the responsibility for passing the food and condiments from end to end. This was done while sitting braced up (at attention) on the edge of the chairs, chin tucked in, eyes in the boat.

Plebes often actually got to eat between recitation of rates (reciting passages, statistics and folklore memorized from Reef Points), sports scores, current headlines from the morning paper, the names of movies being shown in town, and a host of other exercises in mental agility.

It was also a time of physical and psychological testing of the Plebes. The slightest misstatement or procedural error when passing food would result in the upper classmen singling out that Plebe and exposing him to unwanted attention. The more stressed out the Plebe was, the more they would dump on him, ordering him to shove out (sitting without benefit of a chair) or clamp on (doing the same without the assistance of the floor) and other feats that seemed to defy gravity. Clamping on involved suspending oneself on the edge of the table using one's elbows and knees as a vice grip.   Naturally it was hard to pass food back and forth when clamped on.

Plebes were often used to carry messages between upper classmen at different tables. "Mr. Stark, SIR! Mr. DeThomas sends his wishes for a pleasant morning and wants to inform you that your girlfriend left her panties under the bench on Stribling Walk," which was quickly met with an invitation to "come around," or with an escalation of the message traffic: "Mr. Stark returns Mr. DeThomas' greetings and wishes for a nice day and wants to advise him that they were not Susie's panties, but your mother's panties," and so forth and so on. Of course, as in Roman times, the messenger was the one who bore the impact of the message contents.

Go "Wildman" Mr. Bolger, and the plebe would go to that first classman's table and use both hands to muss up Bolger's hair while screaming "Wild man! Wild man!" "Come around, Mr. Zino" would be the reply.

There were amusing times as well: "goody, goody, yummy, yummy, messy, messy, pie eating contests," always with blueberry pie, were challenges where two upper classmen would pit their Plebes against one another, hands behind their backs, the piece of pie positioned on its crust with the acute angle pointing upward. The Plebes would commence a race to see who could consume the dessert the fastest, actually inhaling the delicacy. This would be met with a G_G_Y_Y_M_M_P_E_C challenge from another table, pitting their winner against ours, until the winner could no longer keep the blueberry pie down, let along look at another piece of pie for weeks to come.

Plebes also learned to burble peas. With head pointed skyward, the plebe would suspend a green pea on a column of air exhaled from the mouth with just the right velocity and technique.

Few Plebes looked forward to meals, but knew they were a fact of life. Each one that passed without accumulating more come arounds was deemed a success. Needless to say, the Plebe experience was an ordeal of sorts that had to be faced one day at a time. If you dwelt on it, one could work himself into a state of depression.

Although there was much cooperation among the Plebes, there was also a sense of competition. You would always be observing the other Plebes and say to yourself, "if he can do it, I can do it." Almost like riding the academic "curve," it wasn't the absolute score that counted so much as the relative score. Each episode that passed was another success behind you. With each passing day, there were fewer to come. We all looked forward to June week when we would climb the Herndon monument, replace the "dixie cup" with the Midshipman cap and become Youngsters and enjoy a period of relative calm, concentrate on our studies and sports, and begin to exercise the lessons of leadership that had been closely observed during the year.

Getting through Plebe Year was an accomplishment in which we took a lot of pride. Many of us didn't make it. Some quit, others failed to make the grade either academically or on fitness reports and were asked to leave.

To stick it out you had to want it badly enough, be motivated, summon your inner strength. Plebe Year and the character-building activities that were so much a part of it tested our resolve, our commitment. The Navy didn't want to make the four-year investment in a young man who wasn't serious about a naval career.

That was back in 1963. Much water has coursed the Severn since that time, and many changes have taken place on its shores, many for the better, but not all.

Richard Zino '67

Mealtime Molestation

If you happened to be a Plebe in the mid-1940s, you will recall with mixed feelings of hilarity and horror, the pranks meted out by upperclassmen for your failure to name the members of the U.S. Cabinet in five seconds flat, or the sister ships of specific classes of Navy destroyers - in alphabetical order, no less.

"Shove out, Mister," was the dreaded aftermath of your failure to satisfy your taskmaster. That meant that you had to push your chair out from behind you but maintain a seated position. You were literally sitting on air. And you continued to partake of your meal along with everyone else around the table. Soon, the upperclassmen would turn their attentions to some other hapless Plebe, as your legs began to shake from the strain. Your only salvation was to inquire, during a rare lull in the goings-on, "Sir, am I the forgotten man?" And if your condition of distress seemed sufficiently critical, he might condescend and let you "come aboard." You were glad to be sitting again, but you had lost your appetite.

For lesser mealtime infractions, Plebes were obligated to eat "square meals." You would lift a forkful or spoonful of food vertically from your plate and, at mouth level, guide it horizontally into your mouth. Then you would chew and swallow and return the utensil over the same path back to the plate for another "square" feeding. Of course, this exercise was applicable only for soups and certain vegetables. Forget about cutting any meat with your knife. Square meals were strictly a one-handed operation. If there was nothing but meat left on your plate, the merciful upperclassman might tell you to "knock it off," and you were finally allowed to finish what was left of your meal in relative peace. But a real S.O.B. would finish your meat for you while you were - ahem - otherwise engaged.

Woe be the Plebe who could not "burble" a pea. Whenever peas accompanied a meat dish, such as the ubiquitous "elephant turds" - a week's supply of meat leftovers ground up and served in huge blobs, one per table - Plebes had to make like circus-trained seals. You would select a pea, preferably one that was close to spherical in shape, put it between your lips while lifting your head until you looked straight at the ceiling. Then, ever so gently, you would blow a steady stream of air so as to lift the pea from your lips and keep it aloft about an inch or so above your mouth for an interminable ten seconds. If you managed this legerdemain successfully and didn't collapse from lack of oxygen within the allotted time after lift-off, you were permitted to resume your meal. The less adept pea-burblers inevitably found themselves "shoved out" for failed or aborted missions.

How we didn't get ulcers from these mealtime goings on, is a good question. And looking back, you ask yourself, would I do it again. Oddly enough, the answer is yes. A Plebe may not have been aware of it at the time - he was too busy licking his wounded pride - but he was being groomed as a future naval officer. Shoving out and pea-burbling per se didn't make an officer. But overcoming obstacles did.

Paul Laric '49

Shooting Down the Red Baron

Baron Manfred von Richthoven, the legendary Red Baron, was credited with shooting down eighty planes in World War I before he was shot down himself. During one of our Plebe year Sunday evening "happy hours" in the mess hall we managed to recreate that historic occasion.

To prepare for our presentation, four of us disappeared into our aircraft hanger to change into our flight suits (we went under the table and stuck napkins into our collars). Then, upon emerging, one of us became the field radio announcer and vividly described the exciting aerial combat action. The first two flyers to take off were the Baron, himself, and his first hapless victim who was immediately shot down, complete with convoluted hand and facial expressions and appropriate sound effects.

However, when the next flyer took to the air, the Baron had more difficulty getting into position to shoot. In fact, the Baron was actually out-maneuvered. His airplane was hit and went into a spin, heading for the ground. When last seen before hitting the ground (disappearing under the table), little drops of red tomato ketchup blood oozed from the corner of his mouth. When the upperclass stopped laughing, we got to "carry on" for the rest of the meal.

Bill Patterson '43

Bancroft Hall Catering

Every former Midshipman remembers, among other things, two particular phenomena about their days at the Academy:

· Plebes at the mess hall tables were often so busy answering professional questions and engaging in other similar character-building activities that they rarely got all the nourishment that growing young men in a pressure cooker environment needed, and

· Upperclassmen, unless they were independently wealthy, never had enough money to do the types of things that were necessary to enjoy Midshipman life to the fullest.

During our first class year in the spring of 1965, my roommate Gil Crouse and I thought we had hit upon the perfect solution to both of these problems. We reasoned that, since the sandwich vending machines available to Midshipmen always seemed to be stocked with rather stale merchandise, we could make our own sandwiches and sell them to starving Plebes after the evening meal. To start our little social experiment, we went out into town on one of the few days we were allowed to do so, and bought $20 worth of bread, mayonnaise, mustard, bologna, cheese, and sandwich bags. In those days, you could get a lot for $20. While we didn't have kitchens in our Bancroft Hall rooms, we were blessed with really large desks sized to accommodate two Midshipmen, with one sitting on either-side facing the other-. Recognizing that it might affect our studies, we cleared all the books off our desk and 'sterilized' it with cleanser, so that we could prepare our sandwiches in a clean environment. Being ahead of our time, we figured this would prevent our later being sued by a disgruntled fourth-classman who attributed a particular sickness he picked up to one of our sandwiches.

We turned all these raw materials into fresh, delicious, packaged sandwiches. To make sure we offered lots of choices, we had cheese and bologna, just cheese, and just bologna. Then we borrowed a couple of neighboring Plebes' book bags, since our class had to carry books in our hands, to tote our wares around Bancroft Hall without revealing to passers-by in the corridors (such as company and battalion officers) just what we were doing. On that first night, we never entered a Plebe room without making at least one sale, even though our sandwiches were priced at a nickel more than the vending machines. And we had 100% customer satisfaction because there was no comparison between our sandwiches and those you could get out of the machines. Anyway, we turned our $20 investment into $40 that night.

Having recently completed a class in statistics that showed the affect of a geometrical progression, we figured that after just a few nights of this we could start raking in real money! How else could you benefit both your fellow Mids and yourselves to such a degree? In those days, even first classmen had limited days on which we were allowed out in town, so we had to wait a while for our next step into the intriguing geometrical progression. We took our $40 and doubled the amount of sandwich supplies, made the sandwiches, and sure enough we had $80 in our pockets after that second night.

Thinking this was almost too good to be true, we took our $80 and again doubled our volume of sandwich makings the next chance we had to leave the Yard. We cleaned the desk as before and spread out our bread over the entire desktop. We proceeded with putting the mayonnaise on about two-thirds of the slices, and mustard on the other third. But before we were able to get to dealing out the cheese and bologna, we heard a sharp pair of knocks on our closed door, and in walked the Officer of the Watch, LT Thearle, along with a mate! For some reason, both Gil and I had an extremely difficult time sounding off after simultaneously shouting "Attention on deck!" Needless to say, as anyone who knew Mr. Thearle could attest, he didn't find the picture in front of him all that amusing. We gave the mate our names and learned that, instead of being on the road to untold riches, we had each just earned ourselves a Class A offense. We were then ordered to turn in all of our food to the mess hall galley. Technically, we only lost our $20 initial investment, since the rest of the $80 loss came out of our profits. But we didn't think of it in those terms - we had lost the potential for hundreds of extra dollars.

Six years later, as I was nearing the end of my Chief Engineer tour aboard USS Buchanan (DDG 14), which is another story in itself but outside the scope of this Academy day reminiscence, I learned that a new Commanding Officer was enroute to the ship. The name on the radio message was, much to my chagrin, CDR Thearle! Even though I was to leave the ship two weeks after his arrival, it was with a huge lump in my throat that I greeted him when he reported aboard. Fortunately, he gave no indication of remembering that earlier incident with the sandwiches. I never knew if he had merely forgotten, or if he was just letting the past remain in the past and 1 guess I didn't want to know which of those two possibilities it actually was.

As even more years piled up and members of the Class of '68 gained notoriety, I often wondered if, on any of those nights back in 1965, 1 had sold my sandwiches to the future CNO, Jay Johnson, or to Ollie North, or to James Webb, or to Kendall Pease. But I hadn't the foresight back then to keep a list of my customers.

Dick Zimmerman '65

V

On the strength of one link in the cable

Dependeth the might of the chain.

Who knows when thou mayest be tested?

So live that thou bearest the strain!

I – Day

While I don't remember referring to it by that name, the day we all reported to the Naval Academy to join the Plebe class, get our Navy-issue gear – including a one-minute haircut – and be sworn in as a Midshipman was very memorable.

For the class of '67, induction day was June 26th, 1963. It was an endless day of waiting on line after line. We were processed in assembly line fashion – 1250 of us – filling out forms, being measured for uniforms, trying on shoes, caps, overcoats, drawing book-bags, books, skivvies, M-1 rifles, neckerchiefs, white works, marching boots, et al. After the swearing in ceremony, I said goodbye to my parents and two brothers saying I'd see them at Christmas time.

I had never seen the Naval Academy before that day and everything was new to me. It was a long day being thrust into a strange environment with strangers who would soon become my life-long friends. We spent the evening stenciling our laundry numbers on all our Navy-issue gear, stowing it neatly in our lockers, and packing up all of our civilian clothes for shipping back home. We had lots of questions and were very impressed by any other Plebe that seemed to know his way around. The second classmen who took charge of the Plebe detail were sharp, professional and no-nonsense types. We were assigned rooms alphabetically, so my roommates were Gary Wright and Frank Zito.

That night, about ten minutes before lights out as we were preparing to hit our racks for some shut eye, we heard the second classman's voices shout "Plebe ho! Hit the bulkheads," which translated meant come out of your rooms and brace up with your backs and heels against the wall of the corridor.

We had two minutes to go back to our rooms, grab every piece of clothing we had so carefully stenciled and stowed, and throw them into a large pile in the middle of the hallway. The Plebes were then instructed to toss them in the air, mix them up thoroughly so that all 40 Plebes' clothing were interspersed, scattered widely, and could only be reclaimed by laundry numbers. Just then lights out sounded. Each Plebe had to take an armful of clothes and remove it from the corridor. Everyone had a bit of each other's gear with no names, just laundry numbers. As I recall, my number was 3268. The likelihood of having picked up any of your own gear was slim to none.

It was literally weeks before most of the clothes had been returned to their rightful owner. And if you forgot to stencil one or two garments, well, you were shit out of luck. This episode taught us a couple of important lessons:

¬ To follow orders
¬ The importance of numbers
¬ Be prepared for the unexpected
¬ Attention to detail

Morning meal formation the following day was comical. Many in our squad were dressed in "white works" that were either a few sizes too large or too small. To this day, some thirty-six years later, I still fold and stow my skivvies military style. Without trying too hard I'm sure I can still find a v-neck tee shirt stenciled with "3268," and I would be surprised if some of my Plebe summer classmates couldn't find a memento of that episode as well.

Richard Zino '67

How Well Remembered

The ritual when I reported to the Naval Academy in August 1945 - after the swearing-in ceremony in Memorial Hall and the equalizer fondly known as "the $75 haircut" - took us through the bowels of Bancroft Hall to draw the items of clothing, books and other gear to begin life as a Midshipman.

In one dark corner of the basement along the route was a machine for cutting the stencils with which we would mark all of our gear. The machine was manned by a salty, be-ribboned Second Class Storekeeper who was obviously not pleased to be relegated to the task of cutting stencils for what he viewed as a bunch of snotty-nosed kids - wannabe officers.

He never looked up as I stood before him, but just barked: "Name?" To which I responded: "Shapiro."

How do you spell it?" he asked.

"Shapiro, S-H-A-P-I-R-O."

"Initials?" "S - S. Shapiro." I answered.

"No middle initial?"

"No, no middle initial."

"Junior, Second, Third?"

"No, just plain S. Shapiro."

He finally looked up, fixed me with a stare, and announced: "You'll never make it!"

Sumner Shapiro '49

Editor's Note: Sumner Shapiro is a retired Rear Admiral and the former head of Naval Intelligence.

Bells Galore

Bells, bells, bells. Every day. For four years. You're jolted from your much needed slumber by a merciless ringing of reveille. It resounds throughout Bancroft Hall, but you'd swear it comes right at you from the overhead of your bunk. You've got precious few minutes till the next bell that "invites" you to breakfast formation. If you're lucky, you make formation just before the late bell gets you put on report for weekend restriction with extra duty. The bells don't stop. You've got bells signaling formations for the next class and the next and the next. They blast away for noon formations, more class formations, p-rade formations, evening formations, study-time bells, and finally taps - not a bugle - just bells. And then in no time, there's reveille again.

By the time you've survived Plebe year, you take the bells in stride. But to the bewildered Plebes, the bells are too often harbingers of impending doom. The Plebes must react to them with lightning speed - and that means putting on the right uniform for the next "act." The uniforms must be free of lint, and the shoes must have a mirror-like polish, lest you be marked down as "out of uniform" and subject to crucifixion by some unforgiving upperclassman.

The best defenses against these offensive time constraints, as many a Plebe has found out, are ingenuity and inventiveness. For example, getting rid of lint in record time is not accomplished by brushing with a whisk broom, issued to you as a part of your Midshipman "gear." Whisk brooms pick up lint from one area of your blue uniform, only to deposit it back on another. A much better solution is to pick up lint with adhesive tape that you pilfer from sick bay when no one is looking. It works so well, it even pays to buy it.

As for the mirror-like polish on your shoes, there's a way that will achieve the desired result in half the normal time. It's a matter of strategy not unlike the deceptive maneuver employed by Dewey at Manila Bay. You simply loosen your belt. This drops your trousers a good inch and covers up most of the critical area. Now, all you have to worry about are the shoe tips, actually, the only part of shoes that must stand an inspector's scrutiny. They never look at your heels. So, there you have it. You've done your shoe work in half the time and made it to formation with seconds to spare before the late bell. Yes, Plebe year can be a bitch. But there are remedies. It takes an open mind - one that can stand you in good stead in your later career.

Paul Laric '49

Formations

Morning meal formations, noon meal formations, evening meal formations. If there's one thing a Midshipman becomes expert at, it's formations. Many times I thought that instead of giving a B.S. Degree in Naval Science they ought to give a B.S. in Formations. Between meals, P-rades, duty watches, marching on to football fields and other special events, a Midshipman learns how to dress in the proper uniform, shine shoes, rig a cap, remove a stain from his white gloves, web belt or leggings. He practices daily to knot a perfect tie with a dimple in the middle, check his gig line, and ensure medals, buttons, cap visor and belt buckle are shiny. Talk about being a polished individual, middies, cadets and zoomies are, if nothing else, ready for inspection at all formations.

It seemed at times that appearance is a number one priority, more important than academics, sports and military preparedness, closely followed by punctuality. Midshipmen go to great lengths to look "spiffy" and pass the most stringent of inspections with the least amount of effort. A company mate of mine, Dave Cooper, now deceased, God rest his soul, was among the best at passing inspections with flying colors. He had this pair of shoes that were well-worn and cracked beyond belief. But with a technique all his own, Dave managed to put a good eighth inch layer of polish on these things and they would dazzle the bejesus out of the most ardent drill sergeant. The problem was, he couldn't walk without the wax polish breaking up and falling off in clumps in his wake.

So Dave solved this minor problem by being the first to show up at watch inspections. He arrived with the aide of two Plebes, one on each side of him carrying him a few inches above the deck (floor to you landlubbers) by holding his stiffened elbows. Once there, Dave would stand still and, if he had to move to reposition himself to line up properly, he would do so only by walking very carefully on his heels without bending his feet at the toes.

Patent leather shoes for men had not been introduced at the Academy. Corfam was just being introduced, were uncomfortable and didn't hold a shine well. And, just maybe, Dave didn't want to spring for the twenty-eight bucks that a pair of new Florsheim would cost, which in those days was about two month's worth of pay after the Academy deducted fees for the laundry, cobbler shop, barber, uniforms and the many other services that a Midshipman may or may not have used on a regular basis.

Dave was one of my idols because he never sweated the situation. He'd take his lumps when and if they came, but never worried about it. He didn't sweat exams, room inspections, sports, strength or endurance tests, and – of course – he never sweated the small stuff.

On graduation Dave was commissioned a Second Lieutenant in the Air Force.

Richard Zino '67

VI

When the ship that is tired returneth,

With the signs of the seas showing plain,

Men place her in dock for a season,

And her speed she reneweth again.

Vivid Memories

I've just noted your advertisement in the July/August *Shipmate* and have a short story to share. While it does not exactly exhibit the attribute of having had a profound influence in bringing out the qualities that are unique to USNA graduates, as you requested, it does fulfill another criterion that you list. Namely, it is a rather colorful experience. Here it is:

My most vivid memory of youngster cruise is not of shining brightwork, of which I did plenty; it is not of the words of wisdom spoken to me by my sea-dad - I cannot even remember them; it is not even of the Portland Rose Festival to which we cruised to San Diego for participation.

No, my most vivid memory is that of eight Midshipmen Third Class standing on the quarterdeck while initially reporting aboard the *USS Stein* tied up pier-side in San Diego and watching my classmate, Mark, race for the rails to violently discharge the contents of his suddenly seasick stomach overboard. Youngster cruise was a long one for Mark.

Hope you find this interesting and maybe even publishable.

Winford Knowles '80

Summer Cruise Experiences

My Youngster cruise was spent aboard the *USS Saratoga* (CVA-60) out of Mayport.

We performed duties generally associated with nonrated enlisted personnel rotating between the various departments of the ship. We were assigned stations and participated in all ship's drills and evolutions.

We were berthed in a large enlisted berthing compartment on the 0-3 level aft. Think there were some l/c Mid'n aboard but as I recall, we weren't really in contact with them much. We usually had an E-4 or E-5 in charge of our various working parties.

Lanny Cox '63

3/c Summer Cruise Experiences

Lanny left out a few details...........

We ferried out of Annapolis at Oh Dark Thirty on Graduation Day to pick up the ship in Norfolk. Our cruise director had arranged a surprise for us, as the ship was in drydock. Now that's a sight that will create a lasting impression, a CVA in a bathtub!

When we got to Mayport, they held a formal Ball on the flight deck. All of Jacksonville's finest had been invited to trip the light fantastic with the gentlemen from Annapolis. I managed to corral the daughter of the publisher of the *Wall Street Journal* who threw an impromptu party in her home later that evening for several of us who were about to "go to sea." When they dropped us off at the ship the next morning, we all promised to write and bid them adieu. I thought then, "This is the real Navy."

As Lanny said, we bunked in enlisted quarters, but as a group. I happened to be the MCMO, but most were dispersed throughout the ship's divisions for work assignments. We did have special training sessions now and again. We stood regular enlisted watches. In fact, I'm not so sure that the watches weren't specifically the least desirable watches. You know the type, After Steering, 27 decks below, 117 degrees F, within sight of the CPO air-conditioned shack. By the end of the cruise, all had passed both the Seaman and Fireman tests.

When not on duty, we could roam the ship freely. Pete Browne and I used to slip up to the Secondary Con when we were launching and watch the planes dip and recover. It was like our own private bridge. We could track the planes and the ship's movement on the radar sets that were operational. Unfortunately, the helm was disconnected.

Observing flight ops, particularly at night, was mesmerizing. You could see first hand the skill of the Airdales on the flight deck; smell the burning jet fuel; hear the cables slapping the deck; feel the catapult ram home; and not fail to be inspired by it all.

We lost two pilots over the side; I saw one of them as the helo immediately hovered over the plane, but the pilot had been knocked out and quickly sunk into the Atlantic. The ship was somber for a day or two after each incident. It underscored that this was serious business and not the movies.

Although, I had no intention of going Navy Air, the experience was tremendous reinforcement of the Navy in general and life at sea in particular. I have to believe that a 3/c YP or sailing cruise would fare inferior in terms of training and eventual adaptation to shipboard environment.

P.S. When we returned to Jacksonville, our ladies were miffed that we hadn't written. They wouldn't go out with us again.....for a day.

Patrick Waugh '63

Sweepers, Sweepers!

It was June of 1964, and off to Youngster cruise for the class of '67. I was one of a dozen or so to be assigned to the *USS Bigelow*, DD-942. It was my first experience aboard any vessel larger than a YP. She was a sleek destroyer and we were bound for northern Europe, including port stops at Kiel, Rotterdam, Bergen and Stockholm. You could pay thousands of dollars for a comparable civilian cruise. We were on top of the world.

Our days were filled with watch-standing, general quarters, man overboard drills, training in all departments, and helping to keep *Bigelow* ship shape and seaworthy. It took us 21 days to cross the Atlantic due to participation in a number of fleet training exercises

A basic principle of life at sea is keeping the compartments and passageways clean and ever ready for inspection. Every one of us Midshipmen was assigned a cleaning station. I remember having the "thwartships" passageway forward as my cleaning station. One day the *Bigelow* encountered a nasty storm with high seas and my passageway was awash in salt water. I manned a swab mop and bucket, doing my best to keep the level of water to a minimum.

Despite my best efforts to keep the passageway dry, the sea was washing through the water tight doors each time another sailor headed for the lifelines to "call for Ralph," a euphemism for throwing up over the side of the ship. Unfortunately, I easily succumbed to the nausea that accompanies sea-sickness. Seeing others barf would automatically trigger a sympathetic reaction on my part, and having to clean it up to minimize slipping by shipmates and maintain the cleanliness of my space was quickly becoming a losing battle. The aroma of the noon meal, semi-digested, and now freshly up-chucked, only served to bring on additional heaving. I found myself slipping and falling in the organic slime. What an auspicious beginning to a career as a naval officer.

My cleaning station had now become a two-man assignment. Once the situation was fully assessed, the division of responsibility became obvious. My helper would take responsibility for keeping the passageway clean and ever ready for inspection. My duty was to clean up after myself. I was, in fact, my own cleaning station.

This was an incident that anyone would want to quickly forget and deny ever happened. I managed to get through the rest of the cruise, learn a bit about things nautical, and I even enjoyed time ashore in the ports of call. But otherwise that cruise is a blur.

Fast forward to 1997. I'm long since out of the Navy, but remember my years of service fondly and have turned out for my 30th year reunion at the Naval Academy. Seeing many classmates from my company that I haven't talked to since graduation is great and we spend as much time as possible renewing friendships. At a farewell luncheon, filled with joyous recollections of days gone by, my attention is suddenly distracted when I overhear snippets of another dialog down at the far end of the table. The subject was folk legend of sorts about a Midshipman on youngster cruise who became so seasick and, never quite able to reach the lifelines in time, was assigned as his own cleaning station.

One of my two classmates caught my eye and, with a shit-eating grin, said, "isn't that right?" I had so blocked the cruise out of my mind that I had forgotten one of my closest buddies was also on the *Bigelow* with me and, 33 years later, still felt an obligation, a calling if you will, to help perpetuate the legend of the zero-sum self cleaning station.

Anonymous '67

VII

So shalt thou , lest perchance thou grow weary

In the uttermost parts of the sea,

Pray for leave, for the good of the Service,

As much and as oft as may be.

Liberty In New York

It was the fall of Youngster or Second Class Year. Bodies of U.S. servicemen killed in Europe during World War II were being returned for burial at home. The ships carrying them were arriving in New York, where there would be a funeral parade and memorial services to honor them. The call went out for volunteers from the Brigade to form two battalions of Midshipmen. The parade and ceremony were to be on a Sunday, following the football game on Saturday afternoon against the University of Pennsylvania in Philadelphia. It meant a Saturday night liberty in New York.

Jimmie, my fiancee during the four years that I was at the Naval Academy, and my wife of almost fifty years since, agreed to meet me in New York. You don't get any better deals than that. I volunteered.

Sunday morning, we formed up down on the Battery and marched from there at funeral pace all the way to Central Park. We were at right shoulder arms the entire route - better than three hours, as I recall. What seemed like the entire U.S. Cavalry just ahead of the contingent of Midshipmen made life even more challenging as we attempted to dodge their extremely large and frequent droppings without breaking ranks. By the time we arrived in the middle of Central Park and they finally gave us "order arms," our right arms were so locked in position that we had to pull the rifles off our shoulders with our left hands. We then stood at parade rest for two hours or more while politician after politician took turns at the microphones.

72

Finally, back to the buses for the return to Annapolis. As rough as it was, it was a privilege to be part of the Navy contingent honoring our war dead. And then there was that Saturday night liberty in New York with Jimmie. Who says you should never volunteer?

Sumner Shapiro '49

High Expectations

It was December of 1965, or was it 1966, it's hard to remember. My roommate R.J. "Duke" Armstrong and I had seen a notice on the 4th Battalion bulletin board and submitted our names as military escorts for the International Debutante Ball in Manhattan.

I lived on Long Island, so I was familiar with the "Big Apple." We brought our "mess dress" blue uniforms, all the studs, cufflinks, ribbons and other paraphernalia that goes with the uniform, spit shined shoes and our best society polish and charm with us.

The event was held at the old Astor Hotel on Broadway and 44th Street in New York City. Rooms had been booked for the two of us at the Picadilly Hotel just across the street. We were on top of the world. It doesn't get any better than this.

Remember, this was the height of the Vietnam War and the military was not in favor among young adults, especially young adults of the very wealthy class. Among the young ladies "coming out" was the daughter of Paul Nitze, the then Secretary of the Navy, who was going to be there himself. Talk about rubbing elbows with the privileged few!

I was selected to carry the flag of the State of Rhode Island, which had a nautical flavor to it displaying the word "Hope" under a prominent anchor. Was this an omen? And I would be the military escort for Dede Pray Lorillard of the tobacco fortune fame. I was introduced to Dede and her civilian escort (her boyfriend) who was a tall, dark, handsome, strapping lad, very into the beat generation that had its own lingo, inside jokes and anti-establishment demeanor.

74

The Academy escorts, and those from VMI, The Citadel and other military schools, were a colorful sight to behold, resplendent in their crisply pressed uniforms. I remember sitting at a large 12-person table with four debutantes, four civilian escorts and four of *us*. Coming from the Naval Academy, where we had lived a rather reclusive existence for all of the prior plebe year (and youngster year wasn't much different) I was somewhat out of touch with the culture of my civilian counterparts. I felt like a Martian that had landed on earth to observe human life forms. And I was treated like an ornament.

Came the time for Miss Lorillard to be presented to society. We had had a brief rehearsal so we knew exactly what to do. I stood up and, with all the military bearing I could muster, held the Rhode Island state flag perfectly vertical and followed my debutante and her lover to the center of the large ballroom with all the appropriate music and applause that you would expect for such a prestigious occasion and, of course, the obligatory curtsey by Dede.

And then it was over. Duke, the only other person I knew, was at a distant table somewhere with his group. I had imagined that all of the uniformed participants would be welcomed warmly and receive a token amount of attention, but this was not the case. Throughout the rest of the evening the civilian young adults clustered in small "cliquey" groups with their family and friends and most of the military escorts had to be content with their ornamental role.

At the end of the evening I said goodbye to Dede and wished her well. I made it a point to go over to introduce myself and shake hands with Secretary Nitze. I had thought he would smile, ask me if I enjoyed the evening, maybe introduce me to his daughter who was standing by his side. At very least, I thought he might acknowledge my patriotic commitment to defending the freedoms we hold so dear. Instead, he seemed to look right through me, causing me to wonder if I had committed a social faux pas.

Duke and I wandered around the city for a while. It was good to get away from the stuffed shirts of high society. I had a chance to think about the charade we had just been a part of. Was I wrong to build up my expectations? I actually thought I would meet and become acquainted with people from the upper social strata. But I couldn't penetrate the tight circle of the privileged class. Perhaps in another time, when Vietnam was not such an overpowering influence on our respective lives. Perhaps in other circumstances, where no military uniforms made us stand out like lepers.

Don't get me wrong. I'm glad I volunteered for the event. I'm glad I went. It certainly was an occasion to remember. I learned a few lessons too:

- It's easy to build up your expectations to unrealistic levels, only to be disappointed with what otherwise is normal human behavior;

- The uniform does not necessarily open doors for you and, in fact, may close them at times;

- You can put a fellow into high society, but you cannot put high society into the fellow.

There are probably many more lessons that could have been learned that evening, but I was too weary to pay attention. And that's all I have to say about that!

Richard Zino '67

Guilty As Charged

The time was a pleasant Sunday morning in May, 1942. In the Pacific, Corregidor had just fallen to the Japanese, and gas rationing had been instituted in the United States the week before. The place was Leutze Park in the yard of the Naval Academy. It was a bittersweet moment. I was sitting on a bench on Youngster Cut-off, across from the chapel with my drag, Dabney Rawlings (today my wife of 53 years), saying good-bye. In a few minutes I would head for noon formation at Bancroft Hall and Dabney for the bus depot to take the Greyhound back to college in Philadelphia.

It had been a wonderful weekend. Dabney had come down for the hop on Saturday night -- long formals for the girls and full dress for the Mids. There was no drinking, no riding in cars -- both proscribed with the threat of expulsion -- and even the first classmen like myself had to be checked back into our bunks in Bancroft one hour after the hop ended at 2330. Sunday morning we had attended chapel - compulsory - and then walked in the yard, because liberty outside the gates did not start, even for first-classmen, until after noon formation.

The time together meant a lot to us. In less than a month, I would be an Ensign on my way to the war on board a destroyer in the Pacific. As we got up to go our respective ways, Dabney to her bus and me to muster my platoon, I reached over to clasp one of her hands in both of mine as I told her how much I looked forward to seeing her June Week.

Suddenly, at this moment, out of the bushes behind us rushed a Jimmy Legs -- a civilian campus cop -- with his pad and paper ready. "Mister, what is your name? You are on the report for P.D.A. (public display of affection)." That single indiscretion caused me to be confined to my room for the next weekend. As my Company Commander said, "As a first-classman, soon to be an officer, you should set a better example." Whew!

James L. Holloway, III. '43

Editor's Note: Retired Admiral Holloway is President of the Naval Historical Foundation. He was the 20th Chief of Naval Operations immediately before retiring in 1978. He served in three wars, beginning with World War II, and received three Navy Distinguished Service Medals and two Defense Distinguished Service Medals. A naval aviator, he was captain of the first nuclear-powered aircraft carrier, the USS Enterprise (CVAN-65).

VIII

Count not upon certain promotion,

But rather to gain it aspire,

Though the sight-line end on the target,

There cometh, perchance, a mis-fire.

Fluency in Spanish

My fluency in Spanish prompted me to volunteer for After-Dinner Speaking (ADS) (I believe each language had its own). ADS involved an appearance by Midshipmen, who had volunteered, at an evening event in formal dress. The pluses were the good food, the opportunity to diversify where we had the good food, the occasion to be with different people (Midshipmen from other companies, and some faculty), and the additional chance to practice the foreign language. The minus was the requirement that each attendee deliver an address in the foreign language, which invariably induced in me fears of falling on my face, especially so in a second language. Before I spoke, I wasn't able to attend too well to the addresses of the other speakers. After my speech, I could relax and enjoy the other speeches and the sociability of the evening.

One evening, during my speech, I said (and naturally I'm giving the English rather than the Spanish) "Three aspects (I don't recall what my subject was) were unforgettable to me." And I then forgot all three! Try as I might (and trying, as many of us have learned, harms rather than helps) I could not remember any of the infernal factors I had characterized, not only as unlikely to be forgotten, but impossible to forget.

My pomposity has proved an obstacle in my dealings with others but a saving grace has often been my sense of humor. Here I was able to rescue myself from this mortification by using the debacle to illustrate how I frequently foul myself up by trying (because of my innate insecurity) to appear infallible but only end up with egg on my face. What has become clearer to me the longer I live is that, when my worst fears are realized and I slip, rather than seek to blame it on an outside agent -- the crack in the sidewalk, the banana peel someone thoughtlessly discarded, or, worst of all, my paranoid delusion that an enemy malevolently tripped me -- I should ridicule my clumsiness.

The second incident involving my ability to speak Spanish was the following. During our first-class year, the cruise ship for Midshipmen from Spain, *Juan Sebastian de Elcano*, came to the Naval Academy. As Chairman of the Reception Committee, I was asked to serve as one representative of USNA in welcoming them to Annapolis, and my capability in Spanish made this easier and mutually rewarding. My visit to their ship and wardroom led to the inevitable offer of liquid refreshment stronger than fruit punch which my indoctrination in regs required me to decline with thanks. I was given a tour of their sailing ship, and an opportunity to speak with some Midshipmen and crew, in addition to those officers who received me when I came aboard.

My tour included the astonishing discovery of a cow kept aboard. It was explained to me after I inquired (it isn't often one finds a cow aboard a ship in active service) that the cow was available for the fresh milk it could provide (but how many thirsts can one cow slake?), and for the meat it could furnish when its milk-delivery potentiality had been exhausted. My guess is that, if a Spanish firstclass Midshipman threw a "Mister, how's the cow?" at a Plebe aboard *Juan Sebastian*, the question would not have been academic but expressive of solicitude for the ability of the female of the bovine species to continue the accustomed supply of milk.

Elliott Schuman '49

Editor's Note: Elliott Schuman stood first in Spanish and, slash that he was, was hopeful of capturing the award for highest standing in foreign languages. When the award -- a pair of binoculars -- went to J. E. Draim, a French scholar, Ellie said that, besides disappointment, he felt astonished that someone could know more French than he knew Spanish. Those of us who know him may recall his partiality for analyzing situations and people. He has diagnosed himself as "an interesting clinical example of pretentiousness and insecurity," and seems amply qualified to judge.

Manning The Boards

Dick was a classmate of mine who hailed from Mobile, Alabama. He and I happened to be in the same section of a course in U. S. Naval History during our 2nd class year. Each section consisted of about 12 Midshipmen. We would each draw a slip from the instructor's desk on which was written a question about the day's assignment, man the blackboards, proceed to write our answer on the board, and stand at parade rest until called upon to recite. At that time we were studying the naval battles during the Civil War.

Dick's slip said, sketch and describe the battle of Mobile Bay. When he was called to recite we saw a detailed sketch of Mobile Bay and then he started reading, "The enemy under the leadership of Admiral Farragut...." This brought down the house, including the instructor. Dick went on to describe what a beating the Union forces took. I can't remember whether Dick mentioned "Damn the torpedoes." Anyway we learned that there are different slants to an engagement. I think the instructor gave Dick a good mark.

H. Stewart Moredock '39

Opera BUFFoons

Next to unexciting Midshipmen summer cruises to Guantanamo, Cuba, or Colon, Panama, what could lift a Mid's spirits higher than the prospect of a Mediterranean cruise? Yes, it finally happened and one of its highlights was an event that can hardly be classified as a character-building experience. In fact it may not even belong in this collection of stories with wholesome and purposeful endings. But what a story. I keep re-living it and it breaks me up every time. Maybe it will also tickle the editors Laric and Zino - enough to reprint it, even though it has no redeeming social values, as the saying goes.

The Med was a blast. We climbed the rocks of Gibraltar, then quenched our thirsts with Malaga, the smoothest of Spanish wines. In Cannes, we ogled at bikini-clad demoiselles on the beach, partied at the Carlton and the Casino where we also parted with a few bucks at the roulette wheel.

Next was Naples and a bunch of us signed up for an overnight tour to Rome to soak up some culture after the levity of Cannes. The Vatican, the catacombs, the fountains, the forum and the pasta were all marvelous. But the icing on the cake was yet to come. The opera. And what luck. They were playing *Aida* and the location could not have been more appropriate for this love-tragedy of ancient Egypt: the outdoor amphitheater at the ruins of the Baths of Caracalla, named after one of Rome's more blood-thirsty emperors.

And there we were. A bunch of Mids who were about to be treated to a gala performance in an unbelievable setting. The occasion called for a toast, as we waited for the curtain to rise. An enterprising and foresighted classmate saw to that need and the flask of booze he brought along was passed from one to the other until our spirits soared with the rapidly ebbing level of - I think it was Strega we were getting high on.

The curtain goes up, the music swells and the voices resound in wondrous harmony. Pretending to be seasoned opera afficionados, we nodded to one another knowingly, until the charade became too much and the snickers could no longer be repressed. The audience around us responded to our mirth with angry hisses and "bastas" - Italian for enough. But to us it sounded like name-calling and we didn't like it. "Bastard, yourself," replied big Andy from Texas and the rest of us cheered his true grit. The revelry continued unabated. "Hey, look at that babe with the big... and look at those bow legs and knobby knees on that platoon of lancers." We were really bad.

But then came the climax. Beautiful Aida began her mournful aria, and when, standing amid the ancient ruins, she lifted her arms skyward to dramatize her plight, there emerged from some clouds a propeller-driven Alitalia Airliner that not only drowned the diva's dulcet tones, but sent the rowdy Midshipmen reeling with side-splitting, irrepressible laughter. The modern day aerial intrusion into ancient Egypt was too much for us. And we were too much for the Italian audience. For, in no time a cadre of unforgiving ushers had us marching single-file, but still clowning, out of the amphitheater and into the Roman night. We topped off our cultural evening with a few nightcaps at a friendly trattoria and felt enriched - each one of us from an unforgettable night at the opera. (The Marx Brothers had nothing on us.)

Anonymous

85

IX

If ye win through an Arctic ice floe,

Unmentioned at home in the Press,

Heed it not, no man seeth the piston,

But it driveth the ship none the less.

Class Distinctions

A unique feature of the Service Academies is the system of Classes. Other institutions have their Greek letter societies or their particular school or college within the university. At the Naval Academy you are categorized for the rest of your life by your Class. A new Class is formed every summer and except for those "turned back" from a preceding Class for either academics or some other major cause, the ranks of a particular Class are closed forever. Loyalty among classmates is high. Pride in one's Class to the disdaining of almost all others is the Hallmark of the Class System. Class identification is extremely important. Two illustrations will make that point.

About 1970, after returning from Vietnam, where I commanded a Marine infantry battalion, I was on the faculty of the Marine Corps Command and Staff College at Quantico, Virginia. The Alumni Association invited all Class Presidents and Class Secretaries to a meeting at the Officers' Club at Fort McNair in Washington, D.C. I put on my sincere blue suit and drove the 30-odd miles north.

When I arrived at the club parking lot I knew that it was going to be an auspicious meeting. Orange cones announced that parking spots had been reserved for an ocean of flag and general officers, mostly retired. I finally found a spot a distance away. When I got to the meeting there was a table of name tags and I picked up the one which said, "HAMMOND '51." I noted that the other name tags, as yet unclaimed, was a list of World War II with the original cast.

The meeting was presided over by the President of the Alumni Association, Mr. Hanson W. Baldwin '26, military editor of *The New York Times*. Midway through the meeting a very stylishly dressed elderly gentleman was helped in by two stewards and seated up front. It seemed that he had recently had a stroke but he asked some very penetrating questions. I thought I had recognized him as a retired flag officer (which he was) but I couldn't remember his name.

The meeting adjourned for libations before lunch. I was enjoying a martini as was another gentleman next to me. I said to him, "Sir, you seem to know most of the people here, who was the elderly gentleman who came in late?"

"What elderly gentleman?" was his reply. "Point him out." I did by indicating that the "elderly gentleman" was seated at a table and also enjoying a martini.

I was not prepared for the response from my new-found acquaintance, who said, "Elderly, hell! That's Art Ageton. He's just a kid out of '23 !" Then my friend turned and I could see his name tag. It said, "CHANDLER '11."

# # #

Many years later, we were living in Annapolis after I retired. My oldest son had been graduated and was a Marine Captain stationed on the West Coast. His duties required several trips east and we never knew in advance when he was coming. Our daughter was living with us and managing the silverware, china and crystal department of Garfinkel's Annapolis store.

The week before the Army game, two ladies came into her department and she was making fuss over them. She recognized one whom we used to see at mass every Sunday in the Naval Academy Chapel. I had introduced my daughter to her and explained that she was the mother of a classmate of mine. She was also a Naval Academy widow, her late husband having been in the Class of '17. The lady with her was her sister, also a Naval Academy widow. A third sister and Naval Academy widow lived in San Diego. During World War I, the Ramsay girls lived in the Yard when their father was stationed at the Academy. They dated and married Midshipmen. In the early 1880s, their grandfather, Francis M. Ramsay, '56, had been Superintendent.

"Is your brother a Naval Academy graduate?" my daughter was asked.

"Yes, ma'am! Class of '82."

Whereupon the other sister said, "Oh, my! I remember when the Class of '82 were all old men!"

Time and Classes march on, but it's a continuing line.

James W. Hammond, Jr.'51

Pride Without Prejudice

Volumes have been written about the "good old days" at the Naval Academy. Frankly, when all is said and done, no matter how sweet or how bitter one's memories of Plebe Year are, those, were the good old days.

Mine is a story of revelation. It is also a story of what was a big step for the Academy in 1938. I like to think of it as a small crack in the dam of prejudice--a crack that grew bigger and bigger until the flood of respect for fellow humans finally burst forth.

But let me start at the beginning:

I was born and raised in Chicago. My grammar school population was sixty per cent Jewish and my high school four per cent Jewish. Somehow, I never knew of racial or religious prejudices except what I read in the newspapers. To illustrate: I was elected president of my high school class even though I was one of a four per cent minority.

Being appointed and being accepted to be a Midshipman was indeed a thrill. My big problem in 1937 was to raise the $125.00 required for uniforms, and the $18.00 bus fare to Annapolis, plus about $10.00 or $15.00 for lodging and food just prior to entering. Much of the problem was solved when 1 won "Bank Night" at the (local) White Palace Theater. The rest I saved from my part-time job as a porter at a large food mart, pay--$3.00 per day. It should be noted that the full-time personnel earned $17.00 per week for six days work, 0900 to 1800-- and these were married men with families. In other words, in those Depression years, $150.00 was a lot of money.

It was a thrill to ride the Greyhound bus to Washington, and to spend two days and one night in my nation's capital. And of all places, it was there that I learned of prejudice. When I went to sit in the back of the local bus, I was informed that "Negroes only sat in the rear of the bus." What continues to amaze me even today is that I was introduced to "Jim Crow" not in the Deep South, but in our nation's capital! Believe me, Chicago was not like this. Washington and Annapolis and all of Maryland practiced segregation in one degree or another. For example, restaurants were restricted, beaches were restricted and seating in public buses was restricted. Indeed, the people south of the Mason-Dixon Line harked back to pre-Civil War prejudice.

In 1937, Plebes entered from about early June until mid-August. My entry into the world of "blue and gold" was on 16 July 1937. What a different world this was-- everything was so different, so unlike Chicago's West Side! I liked it: The milk was cool and rich, the food bountiful and tasty, the white uniforms crisp and natty, the rooms large and clean, the air fresh and pure, and Chesapeake Bay filled with billowing sails and motor craft. My Classmates were as thrilled and as bewildered as I was except the wise Navy Juniors and the experienced ex-enlisted men who entered the Academy the hard way. Why, I even liked the Class of '39 who tormented us all during Plebe Summer.

Came the academic year and the first day of the week, Sunday--I learned I had to attend Chapel. I inquired if I really had to attend, because Chapel held an Episcopalian service, certainly not my religion. I was told that Chapel attendance on Sunday is mandatory, and that the only other choice was the Catholic Church Party, which was not a valid alternative for me. If it were this day and age, I'd no doubt protest through proper channels and have a fair hearing ... not so in 1937.

Either I was naive or else I was brave, but I was not going to be forced to attend a church not of my faith. I figured, what the heck, the hazing I received couldn't be any worse than it already was, so I set out to try to correct a really incorrect situation, Plebe or no Plebe.

My activities were restricted to the only free time in town we had, Saturday afternoon liberty. My project was to meet several Jewish families in Annapolis and to meet the local Rabbi. I wanted to find out if there had ever been a Jewish "Church Party." There had not. My next project was to do something about it.

First, I "tested the water." Two Jewish High Holy days occur ill early Autumn. I requested permission to attend Services in the local Synagogue, but to no avail. Why not? Classes were held on those days, and there had been no history of a similar request. I handled the situation stoically and justified it by rationalizing that Academy policy is Academy policy.

One Saturday afternoon, I called on the Rabbi in Annapolis and asked him if he would consider conducting Jewish Services on Sundays. He was most enthusiastic about the idea, and he encouraged me to pursue it, which I did.

My persistence was rewarded: When I called on the Naval Academy Chaplain, William Thomas, I was ushered in to meet a man full of compassion and understanding. Chaplain Thomas immediately set me at ease by stating that, in a way he knew how I felt because here he was, a Baptist minister conducting Episcopalian Services. He agreed we should endeavor to form a Jewish "Church Party," and he would help in any way he could. But, he warned that I should wait until my Youngster Year. He reasoned that there could be resentment among some of the upper classmen, and as a Plebe, I would be fair game. The better I got to know Chaplain Thomas, the more I believed that if sainthood were bestowed on Baptists, he should be first in line.

In September, 1938, Chaplain Thomas gave me a list of those Midshipmen who were known to be Jewish. I enlisted the services of classmate Howard Schoenbaum, and we searched out those men during the free period from after dinner until the start of study hour (about 45 minutes per day). Finally, in November of 1938, we had formed the first Jewish "Church Party" at the Naval Academy.

I like to think that this broke a significant barrier of prejudice. Today there is a Jewish Chaplain at the Academy. Michelson Hall, Rickover Hall and the Robert Crown Sailing Center are all named for Jews and are used daily by all Midshipmen.

Today, "Jim Crow" is dead at the Academy. Today, blacks are admirals and generals, and football heros and basketball stars. Today every man and woman is equal at the Academy, regardless of race, religion or sex.

Indeed, with prejudice set aside, one may say that these (now) are the "good old days" to be regarded with warmth and pride.

Seymour Einstein '41

The Transition

It was the fall of 1943 at West Point, NY. I was present at the Army-Navy game being played there under austere wartime conditions. World War II was at its height and the only ones present in the stadium, besides the Army cadets and the Navy team, were a few thousand local residents from upstate New York. I recall that Navy won the game but I could not say how many of those watching may have later lost their lives in the war. I was in high school then, but in less than two years I would be wearing the uniform of a Midshipman, and the circumstances of the nation and the world would be quite different from what they were in 1943.

As the Class of 1949 assembled VE day had occurred but the war with Japan was still going on. The transition from wartime to peacetime was already beginning. When VJ day came we celebrated with great enthusiasm, including ringing the Japanese bell. After that, things began to change. There were many resignations from the ranks. Michigan replaced North Carolina Preflight on the 1945 football schedule. We boarded the *Wilson Line* boats for Baltimore to watch some home games. In December we took those same boats on the overnight trip to Philadelphia to watch Army and Navy battle for the national championship. But that game was important in another respect. I brought together many Army and Navy officers recently home from combat to help celebrate the great victory that was World War II in the normal location of the football game.

The most painful part of the transition was to convert back to a four-year program. The Class of 1942 graduated right after Pearl Harbor, six months early. The Classes 1943 through 1947 each graduated in three years. In the summer of 1945, following its Plebe year, the class of 1948 was split. Members of 1948A, half of 1948, became second classmen; 1948B, the other half, became Youngsters. There was much resentment in '48B, some of which was deserved. From my perspective in the Class of 1949 I do not believe that the Navy Department picked a very good way of dividing 1948. It used Plebe year class standing. As a result, many younger men who were fresh from high school academics went ahead of many older more seasoned members, some from the fleet. All concerned would have been better served by dividing 1948 strictly by age. At this point, 1949 became the first full four-year class. We had the benefit of having many experienced officers on USNA staff who had seen combat in the war. In addition to many Admirals who had fought in the war, our visitors included General Eisenhower, General de Gaulle, and of course the Commander in Chief, President Harry S. Truman.

As part of the transition, a major adjustment was made to the 1946 Midshipman cruise schedule. In order to accommodate the academic needs of '48A it became necessary to have two identical six-week cruises, which were made to ports on the US East Coast and the Caribbean. In any case, it was doubtful that Europe could have supported such visits so soon after the war. When we did get to England in 1947, we saw London still in ruins from the blitz of World War II. In January 1949 our class marched in the Inauguration parade for President Truman, the first such event since before the war.

As graduates, we did not fight in the great war from which we helped the Naval Academy transition, but we were prepared for the smaller wars which soon followed.

William King '49

Contributing Author's Notes:

[*In 1945 the Navy did not encourage Midshipmen to pursue a career when they demoted a highly visible Captain on the executive staff. The action was taken for technical reasons but displayed a distinct lack of leadership.*

[*Full dress uniforms for Midshipmen were not restored until some time after 1949.*

[*By 1945 the correct way to "about face" the brigade in a large stadium had been forgotten. A bugle call resulted in disaster. Hand signals were required.*

[*The last class of officer candidate school Midshipmen posted at Annapolis completed its work in 1945.*

[*During our Plebe summer, some Italian prisoners-of-war were still being held at Annapolis. They tended the grounds and apparently were no threat as few guards were in evidence. They were awaiting transportation back to Italy and they often waived to passing Midshipmen.*

The Way It Was for the Class of '37

My Plebe year our Superintendent was Rear Admiral Hart. In an effort to demonstrate attention to detail while inspecting the brigade during Saturday noon meal formation, decked out in white service uniforms, Admiral Hart admonished many of us for not having the gold buttons "heads up" while completely missing collar anchors pinned backwards, missing completely, or only one present.

The following year Hart's son was a Plebe. On being prodded about his father's presence at USNA, young Hart replied, "You, sir, have lived with him for two years; I have spent my whole life with him."

During Plebe year back in 1933-34, we were expected to adhere to a requirement that we "come down with something" when stumped by an upper classman's question. Though I became adept at giving ludicrous answers (which had little to do with the question asked) I felt that this practice conditioned one to be evasive when a clear statement such as "I don't know, sir – but I'll find the answer" would be truthful. Not Good! (This practice was obviously corrected in later Plebe years.)

On a 1934 summer cruise aboard *USS Wyoming*, a Midshipman who could be made to respond verbally in his sleep shouted, "Man Overboard," sending the practice squadron into that emergency drill. *Wyoming's* whaleboat was launched with its plug (a tapered stick) out. The coxwain said the duty whaleboat's plug is always in. A well-placed foot avoided disaster. Draining the whaleboat delayed things while we looked for a missing classmate, found in a hammock slung over an ammunition hoist.

One incident I've never forgotten was during sword manual instruction by my Battalion Officer, LCdr L.P.(the "whooze") Wessel, when he said, "Do as I say, not what I do" after impaling his cap on the end of his sword while demonstrating going to "present arms."

Frank Nickols Shamer '37

X

Cans't follow the track of the dolphin

Or tell where the sea swallows roam;

Where Leviathan taketh his pastime;

What ocean he calleth his home?

Legendary Performance

Following an away game of the 150-lb football team in Pottsville, Pennsylvania, everyone who traveled to the game – players, spectator Midshipmen, etc. – found themselves in a neighborhood bar enjoying their victory and some female companionship over "refreshments." The local gals just loved anything in uniform that moved. The exercise was known as "hooking up" and the activities continued out into the cars in the parking lot.

As the time came for the bus to depart for Annapolis with the approach of midnight, one midshipman - a Plebe no less - was caught involved in what appeared to be some heavy petting on the hood of a car, with his hat on backwards, thoroughly engrossed in his activities and totally oblivious of the growing audience surrounding them. The officer in charge of the movement order, who had been very cool about the drinking and amorous activities, asked this Midshipman to straighten his cap and finish up what he assumed was a long goodbye kiss. After several attempts to separate the pair using verbal encouragement, the OIC finally went over and pulled them apart only to discover that the couple was, indeed, coupled. The offending Midshipman was immediately put on report.

Back at Bancroft Hall, word of his exploits in the Pottsville parking lot spread quickly and the young Midshipman received a standing ovation from the entire restriction squad when appearing for his first inspection muster. It had only been a few short days since committing the infraction but his performance in Pottsville had already become legendary.

Tom Williams '88

The First Black N

About 70 years ago the *Reina Mercedes* came to the Academy. It became a luxurious home for senior officers and the prison ship for wayward Midshipmen. One of the early Midshipmen residents gave himself the first "Black N" for his bathrobe. More on that later.

Now, my time. Vice Admiral Shafroth and his family were aboard. He was a football great of the '04s and '08s. I knew his daughter, Helen, to wave to at least. No invitation, of course, to Captain's Mess! We were a couple of decks down in what is best described as a squad room furnished with hammocks and footlockers. The two portholes had been enlarged for ventilation but barred prison-style.

It was rumored, no proof of course, that at an earlier date, a freedom-deprived Middie had loosened the bars, dropped into the Severn, swam across and ran up to the bar by the bridge for a bottle of Kentucky's best. He, naturally, deserved hero status among his grateful buddies.

What we did, every day, was join the regiment for breakfast, day schedule, lunch and return after dinner...marching, of course and, while near Bancroft, subject to songs, rattle of chain, etc.

On weekends we stayed aboard, but we had the use of the foc's'le. Paid back insults to classmates sailing with their gals. It was our exercise area – vocal as well as muscular.

The population grew second-class summer. The popular road to "liberty" was a ground floor room, 4th Battalion, with a window to the steps facing the Armory. The time to go, of course, was quite a while after taps. The route was shadow to shadow, around the side of Thompson

Stadium. Wait a few minutes to spot a hidden Jimmy Legs...then over the wall to visit a crab, or head to Baltimore or Washington.

The occupants of that room, my summer, at reunions still complain about the traffic causing loss of sleep.

Love, of course, was the major stimulant. Once out, ingenuity got you aboard...from the hospital grounds, cycle in with a package prescription or in the back of a car. My love, that year, lived in Annapolis!

As you see, there have been no names; not even mine, although I'm identified easily by some. I'm supposed to be the record holder with 19 "Black N's."

Anonymous

Wild Bill Ellis

Mid'n Ens. Bill Ellis '74, known as "Wild Bill" to his classmates, had a knack of pushing the envelope when it came to indoctrinating Naval Academy tradition in his squad of Plebes. Before departing in mid-summer at the arrival of the second set first classmen to lead S Company, he suggested to Mid'n 4/c Robert S. Goad '77, one of my roommates, that reconning one of the cannons perched on the Thompson Stadium side of Dahlgren Hall might be an appropriate way to demonstrate his initiative.

Never being one to miss out on my company's midnight strolls, I with Bob and several hand-picked commandos set out in the dark to borrow a long plank from the Rickover Hall construction site. We had scouted the site earlier and knew where to look. Having obtained said plank, we schlepped it the quarter mile across Dewey Field in order to keep out of sight of the Yard Patrol and arrived at Dahlgren. We propped the plank up against the 20-foot ledge upon which lay our prize. I posted myself at the key position, anchoring the bottom of the plank on the solid asphalt. Bob took to the air, inching his way up the plank to the summit. Carefully, he eased the cannon off the ledge and onto the plank to the sound of encouraging whispers from below. Once on the plank, though, the little big gun refused to walk. She slipped off our less-than-stable incline and plunged into the asphalt, embedding herself about three inches deep.

Goad was crestfallen. He hurried down the plank to assess the damage. There she stood, a few hundred pounds of solid brass stuck into the pavement at the precise angle of the great Titanic going down before the iceberg in the

North Atlantic. Try as we might, we could not budge her. We had not figured the specific gravity of brass into our equation of motion. So there we were, a night of stealth and danger, and nothing to show for it back at the company area except a few sundry blisters and splinters.

Among its first class and plebeians, the Naval Academy never seems to be without its Ellises and its Goads. Ellis pipes the tune, and Goad dances his merry jig. But the Yard is also never without its wise groundskeepers. And if you return to that same Dahlgren Hall today and look upon those same perches, you will not see a thing. Wisdom placed those cannon elsewhere, out of fourth class reach.

Edward DeRosa '77

XI

Even so with the words of thy seniors,

And the orders those words shall convey

Every law is as naught, beside this one:

"Thou shall not criticize, but obey!"

All Calls

"Hundredth Night," the evening of the one-hundredth day remaining until the First Class graduates, is celebrated by Midshipmen with a well-intentioned evening of Plebe/Firstie role reversal. The First Classmen are demoted and the Fourth Class, who have been taking it from the upperclasses for some eight months at that point, are tasked with running the Firsties for the evening.

The First Class in my Company had a pretty good sense of humor and played right along with the charade. They did their best to remember their rates, chop down the passageways, square corners, sound off, dress up in all manner of uniforms and generally do their best to draw as much attention from the Plebes as they could during the role playing.

While a fair number of the Firsties stood braced up at attention against the passageway bulkheads pretending to be Plebes again, some of my classmates ran around, stopping in front of each Firstie to attack them with questions and subsequently drop them for push-ups.

Though the chance to give back a little of the Plebe system for an evening was enticing a few of my classmates simply grabbed sodas and tried to relax, making feeble attempts to enter Midshipman society by purposefully and nervously addressing every upperclassman in sight by their first name. For most, however, this seemed a futile exercise and we played along with the First Class doing our best to make their brief return to Plebe year as memorable as possible.

The ensuing two or three hours of mayhem was so loud and so intense that I lost my voice completely by the time it was over and the Plebes became Plebes again. Even with so few days left until the end of Plebe year, we still had our rates to memorize, and the very next morning I was scheduled for a chow call and could not say one word. I had no idea at first how I was going to communicate the information I was responsible for. I could find no one to take the chow call from me, so I grabbed a stack of note cards and frantically scribbled the time, place, and uniform for formation, the menu for morning meal, the Officers of the Watch and the major events in the Yard that day.

At eleven minutes to formation, nine of my classmates and I took station at opposite ends of the five passageways that defined our company area. At ten minutes before formation, as my classmates opened up with a roar of memorized information I, like a skilled cue card handler, shuffled my cards in time with my vocal counterparts. Luckily, the first chow call of the day generally served as wake up calls for many of the upperclassmen, and the passageways remained vacant.

I was still responsible for making a five-minute chow call and when I returned to my position and readied myself, a Second Class Midshipman approached. He held a loop of masking tape and used it to brush the lint from his uniform, as it was the custom of many upperclass Midshipmen to do so. He nonchalantly dabbed at his shoulders and chest with the tape, waiting patiently to hear what my classmates and I had to say that morning, and seemed ready to pounce on any one of us for the slightest mistake.

When we opened up at the five-minute mark, I stood silently with my cards again and nervously flipped through them, keeping pace with my classmates.

As I shuffled my deck of rates, the Second Classman leaned over and read what I had written. As the chow call came to a close he asked me who I thought I was and what I thought I was doing. I stiffened up into a tight brace and held the last card out in front of me in a rigid pose of attention, my last hope.

Although his patience with my stunt was visibly strained, he read it and slowly raised. He looked at me and said, "well, all right I guess." He turned and walked down the passageway to formation, continuing to remove lint with his loop of tape.

I had written, "Sir, yesterday evening I lost my voice during Hundredth Night. Very Respectfully, Mid'n 4th Class Conklin."

Jeff Conklin '93

Hundredth Night

Two stories. The first concerns my desire for vengeance; I had singled out two of the first-class occupants of a three-man room for "attention" and regretted that the "night" consisted only of that brief interval between call to evening meal and lights out. When the mayhem started, I realized how fortunate it was that the role reversal was as brief as it was. As the English might have described it "It was bloody bloody."

I raced from my room with a ping-pong paddle but when I saw the offensive weapons some of my classmates were carrying, and was told that R.T. Lawrence was wielding a 6-foot paddle, as a varsity football player would be expected to, I felt naively sheepish. My targeted first-class room had a lineup of determined retaliators, so I concluded that comeuppance would be amply supplied by others who had also been tormented. I spent the remainder of the evening observing retribution in action rather than administering it personally.

The second story concerns my company. One target of many of my classmates (not mine) was a first-classman. Let's call him Gossage. Gossage hid and could not be found. Predictable fury ensued. My guess is that his classmates detested his cowardice more than our class (Plebes at the time) did. Two and a half years later, when we became first-classmen, whom did we find among the Plebes assigned to our company but his brother.

Now, because there were 36 companies, the probability of this occurring on a chance basis is one in thirty-six, or a shade less than .03. Statistical significance is often assigned a probability of less than .05. Because I would judge from the improbability of the event that his assignment to our company was not by chance, then it was intentional, presumably by someone with a desire to see an injustice righted.

I'm told that the brother, if he didn't already know what had happened, was informed and warned to be particularly careful of the way he comported himself. I don't know what happened to him thereafter. My guess is that my classmates who were directly involved (those who had been deprived of an opportunity to get back at Gossage) realized that any persecution of his brother would have been unfair.

Elliott Schuman '49

An Old Tradition We Just Started

Life in the Navy, Marine Corps, and especially at the Naval Academy is filled with traditions and ceremonies. It is our traditions that help make the Navy unique from the other armed services. While as a Midshipman, I was proud to participate in the many customs of the Academy such as Plebe Summer, the climb up Herndon monument, spotting the Chapel dome after Youngster cruise, and going to Philly for the Army-Navy game. As the second semester of my senior year got underway, my classmates and I began to look forward to even better traditions like service selection night, taking the plunge into the Reflection Pool after our last "P-rade," and finally the big "fling" on graduation day.

It was about February when an evil rumor was being circulated that one of these events was going to be canceled. Word through the Bancroft Hall grapevine had it that the Reflection Pool was going to be drained and turned into a garden. "Wait! They can't do that, its a tradition!" "We can't jump into a garden, maybe they'll wait till after graduation," were some of the more common responses to this impending crisis.

Our concerns quickly got the attention of the Academy brass. The Commandant and his Deputy tried to console us by giving us the practical explanation that the pool had long outlived its usefulness and that jumping into the Reflection Pool after the Color Parade was not a very old tradition anyway. This explanation satisfied us for about as long as a New York minute. A tradition is a tradition, no matter how old it is. For years, jumping into the pool helped make a Midshipman's final parade something special. Some would go so far as to say that jumping into the Reflection Pool was sort of like a baptismal into the Officer Corps.

111

Most of us were determined that we were going to jump somewhere, but where? The Dant and his praetorian guard were making it quite clear that any bold initiatives by the Class of '83 about this matter would not be tolerated. It came down to another Academy tradition of listing our courses of action against Admin conduct repercussions. The general feeling was that if we all do it (whatever we decided to do), they could not keep the whole class from graduating. With, that decision made, the big question remained of where we were going to jump? We were like an accident looking for a place to happen.

Some of the options discussed were the Severn River, the new big pool at LeJuene Hall, and even one person suggested the 100 foot tow tank in Rickover Hall, but no one could really agree. It soon became clear that there was going to be no class-wide organization on this subject and that it was going to be left to the Company level or individual initiative. The general attitude was sort of like just wait till after the parade is over and see what the others do.

Being in the Second Battalion put my Company (7th) in a good strategic position to watch the final events of the Color Parade unfold as we had an entire Battalion ahead of us to make the first move. I am proud to say that our First Battalion classmates didn't let us down. The Color Parade was completed with its usual military smartness. As we marched off the field and made our way towards Bancroft Hall, we realized that if we were going to celebrate our last "P-rade," we had better do something soon. We marched past the Chapel and made a column left towards Tecumseh Court when I saw screaming firsties running towards the fountain between Chauvenet and Michelson Halls.

Even after my company was dismissed in T-court, one final moment of confusion existed as we again debated as to where we should jump - "Lets go to the Chauvenet Fountain!" "No, its already too crowded!" "How about the Severn?" "Are you crazy? That river is disease-ridden." Finally somebody yelled, "How about the LeJuene Fountain?", and with a resounding "YEA! Lets Go!" We took off like a bunch of crazed fanatics running towards our objective.

As we approached the fountain, yelling and cheering all the way, we caught the attention of some tourists. They gave us one of those 'now what are these crazy Mids going to do' looks, got their cameras ready and watched as we were about to do our thing. We formed a circle around the rim of the fountain and on the count of three took the 'Nestea Plunge.' The exhilaration of the moment overcame us as we washed away our demerits of the past and cleansed ourselves for our commissioning.

We played in the fountain for about a minute when it seemed like the entire Second Regiment was charging toward us. We got out of the fountain so they too could take the plunge. After we stepped out, we were still elated giving each other hugs and congratulating ourselves that we, the 'boyz' in 7th Company, were the first to jump into the LeJuene Fountain. Classmates of the Second Regiment followed us in and later, those we were leaving behind, in due time, would also follow. Thoroughly soaked, I made my way back to my room with a contented smile with the knowledge that in my final hours as a Midshipman, I had helped start an old tradition.

Luke Koeller '83

Window Closing Duty

Back in the mid-1960's, and very likely for eons before then, there was a practice observed at he Naval Academy, somewhat subservient in nature, but widely accepted nonetheless. It was called Window Closing Duty. Each week, on a rotation schedule, a room of Plebes (usually three to a room) would be assigned responsibility for closing windows for all of the upper classmen in their company, roughly 35 rooms.

It was the general rule that Midshipmen like to go to sleep in a cool room, but hate to step out of their rack in the morning onto a cold deck. This seeming dichotomy was managed using Plebe labor.

At about 0430 hours (4:30 am) the assigned room of Plebes would wake up and begin their duties by quietly entering each upper classman's room, making their way over to the windows, and silently closing them. This task was not as easy as it may sound at first telling, because it was pitch black dark, the window blinds were usually lowered, and there were often hidden obstacles between the door and the windows, such as books, trash cans, shoes, and wires to radios or stereos.

Should an unfortunate Plebe inadvertently awaken a slumbering upper classman, the punishment would be another come around to add to their schedule of character building activities. In fact, some upper classmen would intentionally place obstacles in the path of the window closers to cause them to make noise. Many a Plebe has spent several minutes holding his breath while hiding in the shadows of a second class room after making a sound and hearing one of the occupants of the room roll over or become semi-conscious.

During my Plebe year, the "Savage" 16th company occupied the 4th deck of the 4th wing of Bancroft Hall. This is the uppermost floor, characterized by a mansard roof and dormers. Some of us window closers would succeed in avoiding the potential pitfalls of hidden obstacles by choosing to close the upper class windows from the outside, walking on the narrow ledges between slanted roof and crown of the outside wall, some five or six stories above ground level depending on which side of the wing you were working.

The window closing chores were accepted by the Plebes because they knew that, for the next three years, each new class of Plebes would take their turn performing this duty on your behalf. It was a very visible sign of becoming an upper classman to be on the receiving end rather than the provisioning end of the window closing activities. I never thought to ask how long this tradition had been going on at Bancroft Hall. We all knew it must have been for generations and that it would surely survive many more.

It was ten or 15 years later, while visiting the Academy one autumn day, that I went up to a Midshipman in the Yard and asked him about the Bancroft Hall routines, among them window closing duty. It surprised me that, not only had he never participated in such an activity, he had never even heard of it being done.

So much for traditions!

Dick Raaz '67

XII

Saith the wise, "How may I know their purpose?"

Then acts without wherefore or why.

Stays the fool but one moment to question,

And the chance of his life passeth by.

Fire the gun, Toot the whistle, And all that jazz

Now, a half-century since Plebe Year, my Reef Points is dust and I have no idea what happened to my wonderfully warm reefer, my youth, or even my #3 set of Jakie Reed blues. But some of the grand nonsense we indulged in at table for the entertainment of the first class is as fresh as ever in my failing brain. Particularly sharp is the recall of Man Overboard Drill, for it led to an extraordinary coup in 1952 over a pack of mischief-bent inspectors from the shore establishment.

As practiced in the Midshipmen's Mess in 1947, the drill had apparently not changed since the early days of steam in the nineteenth century. It consisted then (and I wonder if it survives today) of assignment by a firstie of a Plebe OOD, Quartermaster, and Boatswain's Mate, plus Coxswain and Oarsmen of the lifeboat, who would all go through the long outdated man-overboard evolution of an earlier era.

When the firstie gave the signal. "Man Overboard!" the OOD had to yell out a string of orders at maximum volume. Here's how it went-and please remember that all hands had to say or sing their lines in the shortest humanly possible time.

Firstie: MAN OVERBOARD, PORT SIDE!

OOD: Left full rudder all engines stop; fire the gun; toot the whistle; break
and dip the five flag; Quartermaster, keep your eye on the man.

QM: Quartermaster, aye-aye.

OOD: Boatswain's Mate, Boatswain's Mate, where's the Boatswain's Mate?

BM:	Boatswain's Mate, aye-aye.
OOD:	Boatswain's Mate, call away the lifeboat.
BM:	Man the lifeboat! Lower away! Out oars! Ready all, row!
Oarsmen:	(They make simultaneous rowing motions as they sing) "Oh, the lifeboat crew are we, and we sail the ocean free, for we're members of the lifeboat crew.
BM:	Oars. Toss oars. (To the OOD) Sir, the man is recovered.
OOD:	(To firstie) Sir, the man is recovered.

If the job were well done, the firstie would give us a "Carry on;" if not, a bawling out and we'd sit at attention until the march-out bell.

As I was quite visible at 6'-3", and also, "talked funny" (softly and languidly with a thick Georgia accent), I was frequently favored with the assignment as OOD in these drills.

Since my commands tended to he gracious, slow, and inaudible, my stewardship as OOD seldom--all right, never-- led to a "Carry on" afterwards, which became a matter of concern to my classmates at that unlucky table.

I can still hear that firstie: BELLOW! Mr. McIntosh-- KNOCK 'EM TOGETHER! And SPEED IT UP! Your mouth's full of cornmeal mush!"

Gradually I did improve, until I could rattle out the commands almost as well as the speediest of my Yankee classmates who suffered no cultural impediments in their own speech.

SHIFT FORWARD NOW TO FIVE YEARS LATER, when as an Ensign I was plucked from a big transport (APA) to replace an officer suddenly transferred out of a tiny LSMR in Little Creek, Virginia.

LT. E.J. Plante was the commanding officer, with another LT as XO, a LT. as First Lieutenant, a LTJG as Supply Officer, and me as the new Ops Officer. I reported aboard on Sunday, and Monday morning we were to depart for a three-day Operational Readiness Inspection (ORI).

The Little Creek inspectors were reported to be mean as hell, and given to playing all sorts of tricks on the wretched LSMR's and LST's that nearly everyone else in the Navy held in contempt. When the inspecting officers and men--scowlers and growlers every one--boarded early Monday, we got underway immediately. Thus, I got to meet the inspecting officers and my wardroom shipmates simultaneously.

Oh, yes, and I also got the word that I had the 12-16 OOD watch, having qualified simply by reporting aboard a ship with but two other watch-standing officers.

As my first duty the XO had ordered me to stay out of everyone's way, so I hung around the flagbag on the conning tower all morning, and watched as the inspectors imposed casualties on both the equipment and the crew. They measured our performance with stopwatches, shaking their heads sadly and more or less continuously as they wrote on clipboards.

After lunch the inspection continued, and I went back to the conning tower to take over my first OOD underway watch. I was unaware that the Chief Inspector had selected me, as the junior watchstander, to be the OOD for the required man-overboard drill. I was also unaware that as I lolled over the conning tower rail, viewing the sparkling sea, my CO stood behind me chewing his nails as he saw his career about to go down the tubes.

"MAN OVERBOARD, STARBOARD SIDE!" came a sudden, stark call from the deck aft. Paralysis seized me. I knew nothing about the LSMR. Not how she steered, her speed, turning circle, what kind of engines, how many screws --nothing.

You can guess what happened. Bone-ingrained habit took over and I started BELLOWING at HIGH SPEED the old drill. "Right full rudder, all engines stop!"

A voice I took to be that of Davy Jones boomed hollowly up from the depths, echoing the orders. It was the voice tube from the steering station, one level down.

"Fire the gun; toot the whistle; break and dip the five flag!" I ranted on at max velocity. As the single 5"-38 was buttoned up with all the ammo locked below decks, no one fired anything. (Anyway, that part had originally been to alert ships astern, long before radio.) The same sharp helmsman now yanked the whistle cord six times. An equally on-the-ball signalman broke the "0" flag, probably thinking I'd called for the decades-obsolete "5" flag out of "Ensign's funk."

"Quartermaster, keep your eye on the man; Boatswain's mate, Boatswain's mate, where's the Boatswain's Mate?" The Quartermaster piped up with "Aye-aye, sir." By some miracle, a Boatswain's Mate now stepped forward and also said his lines precisely: "Boatswain's Mate, aye-aye, sir."

"Boatswain's mate, call away the lifeboat." Well, we didn't have a lifeboat, but we did have a motor whaleboat, and it happened to be hanging loose from the davits for maintenance, so the Boatswain's Mate shrugged and yelled over the side of the tower to the oil-stained crew working in the boat to lower the %$&!! thing and go get the @#%! dummy.

By then, with engines stopped and the rudder full over, we had turned a quarter circle and slowed 'way down. I had a moment to look around, and noted with pleasant surprise that with our shallow draft the stiff breeze was drifting us rapidly down on the canvas "man." The whaleboat was already there, and the bow hook was leaning out to grab hold.

I didn't hear anyone sing the lifeboat crew's rowing song and of course there were no oars to toss; nevertheless, in jig time the whaleboat veered over to us to be hoisted aboard and the dripping dummy brought to the conning tower by a grinning Coxswain.

I saluted the Chief Inspector, an iron-jawed old CDR. "Sir, the man is recovered." He glared at me but then, in another miraculous coincidence, he gave the scripted approval by barking, "Carry on, Mr. McIntosh!"

Late Wednesday afternoon, we returned to Little Creek, and the hell began as the inspection party read page after page of criticisms and black marks. Poor Skipper Plante's head was hanging low as the Chief Inspector railed about such things as the wad of waste paper he had stuck behind the latched-back wardroom door Monday afternoon, that was still there Wednesday afternoon.

He concluded, however, by saying something like: "But, Lieutenant Plante, never in my long career have I witnessed such a performance as your newest officer gave as OOD Monday. I congratulate you on your junior officer training program, which I hope you will share with us in an official communication. Your elapsed time of five minutes, forty-five seconds, to recover the man overboard has set a new record for Amphibious Force Atlantic!"

For the next couple of days, the Captain didn't quite know what to make of me, or what assignments to give me. Soon enough, though, he found my feet to be of common clay, and happily figured out my first assignment.

It was to write the report requested by Amphibious Training Command detailing the super junior officer training program that had enabled one of his officers to set a new seamanship record. That really was my first venture into creative writing, which I subsequently discovered to be one of the more useful assets of a versatile Naval or Marine officer.

Vast and well-remembered Plebe knowledge, however, might arguably run it a close second.

Charles McIntosh, '51

Animal Crackers

In 1945, my Plebe wife (roommate) Bob Salomon and I had an "inboard" room on the fourth deck of Bancroft Hall, overlooking a courtyard, euphemistically called "Goat Court."

On almost any day we were assailed by the indelicate odors of Bill, "the X squared." Our comments on our reaction to this hollow-horned ruminant mammal of the genus, Capra, were as indelicate as the odiferous invasion of our olfactory organs. In other words, we were upset with the disgustingly objectionable stench!

When Bob continued to complain, I suggested that since we were being trained to be men of action, that "we" should help our situation by giving this offending mascot some "sanitary salvation." Bob, known to be quick on the trigger (also known as "the impatient Brooklynite"), ran to the sink, filled a bucket with water and with the skill that had distinguished him on the baseball diamond, fired his H_2O missile. Voila! A direct hit from an altitude of four floors! We were overjoyed.

Our elation was short-lived and interrupted by a loud knock on the door and a stentorian voice that boomed, "Are one of you Plebes responsible for throwing water on the goat?" Midshipman Salomon, also known as "Honest Abe," admitted to being the perpetrator. "Report to the Company Commander on the double!"

When Bob was interrogated, the "CC" asked, "Mr. Salomon, don't you like animals?" Bob said, "Yes, Sir, I have a dog at home." "Do you throw water on your dog, Mr. Salomon?"

Bob answered with more honesty than foresight, "Yes, Sir, all the time!"

Bob later had trouble with his knees and we attributed this, at least partly, to the many hours of marching extra duty as penalty for his impulsive attack on Navy's beloved (but definitely malodorous) mascot.

Harvey Conover '49

DeMystifying the Occult

At USNA, it was a matter of urgency, especially to Plebes, either to have, or to ascertain the correct answers to any questions asked.

When our class joined the Brigade the very first day following the relative picnic of Plebe Summer, my classmates and I were confronted by various exigencies. We had to endure shoving out, to play principal roles in such productions as having to summon pigs at maximum volume (as well as to role-play the acknowledgments of the orders with a "Pig, aye-aye"), and to furnish the answers to all manner of mind-bogglers.

One of my very first introductions to the rite of passage to youngster-hood, that made it appear unlikely ever to be attained, was the question "What time did *Exeter* fire her port torpedo?" Not only was I interrogated about something that had hardly even registered -- the Battle of the River Plate between two British destroyers or frigates, I forget which, and I believe a German pocket battleship -- but what was demanded of me was the precise time the port torpedo was fired. A fair enough question. "I'll find out, sir" was the obligatory response. "Well," the first-class Grand Inquisitor continued (I was hardly off the hook), "if you don't know what time the port torpedo was fired, surely you recall (he was a jovial life of the party) when the starboard torpedo was launched." Another obligatory response.

The torture continued. I was asked, among other questions from this particular first-classman at my table, many more details about the engagement on the Rio Plata that took place around 1939 or 1940 off Montevideo,

Uruguay between *Ajax* and *Achilles* and the German ship that might have been the *Graf Spee*. Being lazy, I have not researched it even for this tale and I certainly wouldn't a second time after having been compelled to do it when the members of my class were the duty patsies. You've probably heard the joke about "It could have been worse." Anyway, I suppose I could have been asked at what time the First Lieutenant of *Ajax* expectorated phlegm before the engagement began, or what his grandmother had had for breakfast that morning (or five months earlier). Original sources would have been more difficult to locate, however.

My parents much later informed me how depressed I had become by the running during Plebe year, and the depressing effect my depression had had upon their depressions.

While my memory fails me about other details of the River Plate engagement, the answers to the two questions, as I now recall, were 6:42 A.M. and 6:48 A.M. Historians and debunkers are invited to do the necessary research. I would be interested in receiving the data, even if they expose my descent into senility, dementia, or Alzheimer's, at least one of which has already begun.

One of the obscure bits of mental flotsam I had committed to memory was the location of the brick that had three letters carved on its surface, not far from the right-hand cannon (as one faced Bancroft Hall) with the initials as I somewhat less vividly recall as CIR. What was maddening was that I was never asked. It's deflating to be asked and, initially, not to know. But it's infuriating to know but never to be asked. I was never asked "How is the cow" or, so far as I can recall, any of the other questions that appeared in Reef Points.

When I returned to the Academy with my son, Ken, I looked forward to seeing whether I could still find the brick. But either I couldn't or, what is more likely, it had been replaced. Life moves on. Buildings appear that weren't there before. New people appear, too. The other side of the coin is that people we once knew disappear, and are elsewhere.

Elliott Schuman '49

Postscript to DeMystifying the Occult

I am ashamed, I say again, ashamed to admit that, lazy as I am, I succumbed to superego pressure and researched the part of the previously submitted article that concerned the River Plate engagement.It took place on December 13, 1939. *Graf Spee* (Captain Langsdorff, commanding), German pocket battleship with 11-inch guns, was engaged off Uruguay, between Montevideo and Maldonado, by 8-inch British cruiser *Exeter* (Bell), 6-inch British cruiser *Ajax* (Woodhouse), and 6-inch New Zealand cruiser *Achilles* (Parry). *Graf Spee*, badly damaged and unable to remain in Montevideo Roads without facing internment for the duration of the war for both ship and crew in neutral Uruguay, was scuttled on December 17.

Exeter's starboard torpedo was fired first, at 0632, port torpedo at 0638. Both missed because of evasive maneuvers by *Graf Spee*. My recollected times were off by 10 minutes each, and I reversed the port and starboard tube firings. At least it was *Exeter*. You retain some (faculties), and you lose others.

If, when we meet, I show obvious signs of deterioration and probable dementia, lie and tell me how well I look, and how alert it is obvious that I still am. ...

Elliott Schuman '49

XIII

Do they growl? It is well; Be thou silent,

So that work goeth forward amain;

Lo, the gun throws her shot to a hair's breadth

and shouteth, yet none shall complain.

Thank you, Ingrid

After experiencing a lackluster Youngster cruise to Newport, Panama and the inevitable Gitmo (Guantanamo), word that our 2nd Class cruise would take us to Scotland, the Scandinavian countries and England, was welcomed by all of us with eager anticipation. And just when we thought that this bit of good fortune couldn't be topped, there came a real bonanza. Those Midshipmen with relatives or close family friends in the countries to be visited may apply for an extended (72-hour) shore-leave and visit with their local kinfolk or friends. Wow! What a sweet deal!

My classmates and I, embarked in the carrier *USS Randolph* (CV-15), were eager to take advantage of this one-in-a million opportunity and began wracking our brains and searching our address books for plausible leads that could possibly be relatives or friends. No such luck in my case. But then I remembered some words of wisdom passed down to me during Plebe year by a salty, devil-may-care upperclassman: "You rate everything that you can get away with."

After a little soul-searching, I decided to follow that lead, invent an uncle and aunt in London and bear the consequences. I certainly didn't want to miss out on a few days - and nights!! - of pleasure which London, with its theaters, nightclubs, dance halls etc., had to offer.

Coming up with names of bogus relatives was no problem. But a believable address was something else. As luck would have it, a couple of days out of Portsmouth, the evening movie on the hangar deck was "Gaslight," starring

Charles Boyer, Ingrid Bergman and Angela Lansbury. A fun, if sinister, movie. But what solved a problem for me was right there on the screen. Boyer was driving Ingrid insane so he could, unbeknownst to her, put his hot hands on the family jewels which were stashed away in the loft of her family's London townhouse at 9 Thornton Square. What a perfect address for my London relatives, I thought. I used it in my application for extended leave - and (I must now shamefacedly admit) it worked.

London was everything I expected, and more. I have since returned several times to the scene of my crime, but never enjoyed London quite as much as when I first visited there ... on borrowed time.

Anonymous (for obvious reasons)

Remembering Mo

When we were on the Mo, as you'll recall, we had several 16-inch practice firings, at least one of which was a full, nine-gun broadside. A classmate, name now forgotten but he must have been an idiot like me to do what we did, agreed to join me for a climb up the outside of the lookout tower to a small platform about 2/3rds of the way up. There was no real ladder, just small narrow rungs welded onto the tower. Well, we got up there and made ourselves comfortable, leaning back against the tower, with our legs dangling over the forward edge of the tiny platform.

I recall it as being late in the day, calm, no wind, and the sky turning red and orange near the sun descending near the horizon (though this may just be my active imagination decorating the facts).

GQ for the gunnery personnel was sounded and the decks cleared. After awhile, the turrets ground 'round in their barbettes, and after a further while, the guns elevated to the position the director commanded. All was ready for firing at the sled many miles abeam.

You may also recall that in the barest instant before firing, the firing signal, a "beep-beep" not unlike that of the cartoon Roadrunner, sounded. I remember hearing that beep-beep clearly, after which the universe disappeared. There was a roar, not a bang, but it seemed to go on increasing forever. At the same time, a cloud of choking smoke and very hot air blasted past us, almost blowing us off the platform. There was the smell and taste of the gunpowder, which was strangling and acrid. Simultaneously, also, handfuls of shredded, blazing, cord (from the bottom of the powder bags, I suppose) were flung against us.

As the cloud slowly cleared, we began to see the ship again, but our faces were blazing hot and I thought we were blistered (we weren't, quite), and neither of us could hear a thing. We were both trembling wildly, of course, and it was some time before our nerves were strong enough to brave that perilous climb back down that tiny stack of thin rungs. It was pretty dark by then, so we weren't caught. Naturally we both kept our traps tightly shut---at least, I did.

But I wonder who that other Mid was, and if he ever thinks of that adventure today.

Charles McIntosh '51

Hearing from a Shipmate

Yep, I do remember the "Mighty Mo" as well as the New Jersey, boats that I was lucky enough to "serve" on as a shit-coolie. Remember that phrase?

In fact you give me a chance for a sea-story. On my first Youngster cruise, with Class of 1950, I was assigned as the rangefinder operator on the top of the boat's main battery director.

Being one of the few who for some reason or another could "see" in stereo. I was able to use that skill as a passcard to avoiding most all special and dirty details. That particular skill or trick was very valued, one had to "practice" the skill a lot, and was most important to the gunnery officer who had some sort of competitive gunnery exercise that had to be fired using the visual rangefinder ranges, AND SPOTS.

Would you believe it! There were only two guys on the entire ship who passed the several tests to qualify to take part in firing exercises, me and an old chief (who couldn't get atop the ship when his legs were sore). So, other than seeing the main battery fire a salvo of 9 railroad cars, I also have the honor of participating in a battleship gunnery exercise and actually calling the spot for single-gun firing exercises...and then flunking retest in Calculus!

Bill Aston '50

XIV

Do they growl and the work be retarded?

It is ill, speak whatever their rank;

The half-loaded gun also shouteth,

But can she pierce armor with blanks?

Taking Charge

As I exited Mitscher Hall and into the blistering heat of the July afternoon, I placed my whiteworks "dixie-cup" back on my head and took my place in the platoon formation. My company had just completed one of its many indoctrination lectures, which were the norm for Plebe summer, in the auditorium there. We were now being rewarded with scheduled personal time for the next fifty minutes and were eager to get at it. Despite the heat inside Bancroft Hall to which we were headed, a Plebe's free time is golden, and a minute wasted is too precious to lose!

We waited patiently at parade rest for probably about two minutes; writing letters, studying rates, shining shoes, and polishing brass were beginning to take priority.

"Hey, Fred, why don't you march us back?" a voice asked from the squad behind me.

Why he was so spontaneously selected to be our designated firstie escaped me, but I suppose Fred Adams was itching to get back as much as anyone else. His year of experience at the Naval Academy Preparatory School probably qualified him for the job as much as anyone. He strode to the front of the formation, tucked his Reef Points into the front of his trousers and began to call us to attention. His orders for facing movements and marching were flawless as we called cadence all the way back to our 3rd wing-3rd deck rooms, breaking step only on the metal stairs that wound over the top of the Mess Hall.

Relieved to be back, most of us set about our business without any thought of not having waited for one of our first-classmen on detail, whether it be squad leader, platoon leader, or even company commander, to come and retrieve us. This oversight was soon to become an issue.

"Hey, mate! How the hell did you all get back here?" the voice of Midshipman-Ensign Tony Gurnee resounded down the passageway. The company mate of the deck gave a mumbled reply I couldn't make out.

"What? You've gotta be kidding me! 30th Platoon! Plebe ho!" he shouted and just as quickly all of the Plebes present hit a bulkhead outside their rooms.

By this time, another squad leader, John Dickman, had been informed of the appalling situation: that a platoon of Plebes had taken their own initiative. Bound by the honor code and with several requests for permission not to bilge their classmates denied, my company mates finally gave enough information to recount what happened.

"Who the hell do you think you are, Mr. Adams? Some kind of a stud?" I vividly remember Mr.Dickman demanding of Fred.

"No, sir." Fred loudly responded.

All answers and even requests to explain ourselves could not satisfy the apparently shocked upperclassmen. A general, first-class reaming was in order. Mr. Dickman collapsed against the opposite bulkhead with an "Oh, my God!" and buried his head in his hands. We were eventually ordered to fall out but could hear the gossip outside our rooms as word passed among the Plebe detail regarding what their platoon had just done. Our punishment at the time was to brace up until morning quarters the next day.

The real punishment, however, came later; I, as well as some others, probably realized it as a set-up. We were being marched (by a firstie this time) back from another instruction period when midshipman Ensign Bubba Turman interrupted our cadence as we approached our company area in the Hall.

"'84 stinks," he interjected, and began to repeat.

Bill Derohe, a Bostonian with the same cockiness as the people from that area two hundred years earlier had had, was quick to retaliate and escalate, "'81 sucks!"

Slowly, we all began to pick up the cadence as we rounded the spiral staircase in the 3rd wing of Bancroft, "'81 sucks"-stomp-"'81 sucks"-stomp. By this time Mr. Turman was mysteriously quiet or at least drowned out, and we reached the company area where there were plenty of first-class witnesses. A lecture over insubordination with a stress on respect for other classes as well as fellow shipmates followed, almost as if it had been prepared. We were all on the same team, regardless, we were told, and such a blatant disregard for our mentors would not be tolerated. An all-star come-around was unanimously decided upon by our detail.

Taunting from the firsties over the next couple of days leading up to the evening come-around was best evidenced by my squad leader, Mr. Gurnee, having us sing, to the tune of Tom Dooley:

"Hang down your heads, poor Plebers,
Hang down your heads and cry.
Hang down your heads, poor Plebers,
Oh, boys, you're gonna die!"

As the moment arrived, the worst first-class flamers on all of Plebe detail were present and ready to intimidate. Most had bayonets or baseball bats with them for the purpose of asking us rates, drilling us, bracing us up with our covers under our chins, and an all-out yell-fest. My thoughts at the time were that it won't be that bad; I was sadly mistaken. The all-stars were a nightmare team! We began it all with the singing of *The Star Spangled Banner*, then they started in on us. The building of character comes in many forms, shapes, sizes, and at various moments. Sometimes you just stumble or even march right into it.

"Good God, let's play ball!" a firstie from Port Battalion shouted as he moved with the others in towards us, captivated against the bulkhead. By the end of it all, I was almost to the point of tears. One of our firsties had maintained beforehand that we must all come away from the experience with honor. From the feedback we "walking wounded" received from them, we had done just that and were on our way to "coming aboard."

David Hoover '84

Black Jack Scoville

Academy life, as we knew it in the early 60's, was somewhat more "monastic" then it is in the 90's. Consequently things that happened to us on the Yard as Mids seemed to have a greater impact and stuck with us longer.

Straggling to class while marching was in full swing the second half of our Youngster year (fall of 1960) and it was a wonderful feeling to have some independence in an otherwise very controlled environment. As was customary at that time, the "uniform of the day" was dutifully announced early in the day and that is what was expected of all of us; woe to those who transgressed.

During this time there was an infamous Company Officer (14th I believe), lovingly named "Black" Jack Scoville who was known to fry, literally, at the drop of a hat. He once fried a watch-stander for dust on his shoes.

It was one of those typical fall, maybe rain days in Annapolis but the uniform of the day was "wear raingear." Black Jack was the OOD and was dutifully standing in front of Tecumseh watching all of the Mids wending their way to another day of Bull, Skinny and Steam. As I was rounding the corner between the cannons of "T-Court," I saw Black Jack point towards the bandstand area, which sent the Mate of the Watch off at full gallop in that direction.

As I followed the pointing finger I saw, in the mass of blue uniforms, one solitary figure not wearing his raingear. This individual must have had a sixth sense, because when the mate was about half way to him, he turned around to see the mate running towards him. There was no doubt in his mind who the mate was after --- the one without the raingear! This individual immediately took off running towards the academic buildings (Sampson Hall et al.)

Everyone who was going to class at this time came to a stop as this chase scene unfolded. It appeared the targeted Mid was going to make it to freedom, and you could almost feel everyone in the yard rooting him on. But, as he approached the road in front of the museum, he dropped his books (no fancy book bags for us). Then the most amazing part of this whole scene took place. Everyone in the yard watching the chase let out a collective moan when the Mid dropped his books and the mate caught up with him! You'd have thought it was the star Navy receiver dropping the winning pass at the Army-Navy game.

I've often wondered if Black Jack fried the individual for leaving the scene as well as for the missing raingear! But knowing Black Jack's perverse sense of humor, he probably enjoyed the chase scene as much as the rest of us.

Five years later, I'm a Lieutenant, weapons officer of a DE in Newport, R. I. Black Jack is now a Des Ron Commander with his flagship moored alongside my DE. When I saw Black Jack walking down the starboard side of his flagship, I actually caught myself adjusting my tie, brushing off my blues and checking out my shoes! Some memories really stick with you!

Peter D. Quinton '63

The Good Thing About Raingear

Two events happened to my roomie, Dick Macke, and me during our Plebe years, and neither would have predicted the success we both realized in our Navy careers, albeit his far outshines mine. The first occurred during our first away football game against Maryland held in Baltimore. After five months of being without feminine companionship, we both were eager to meet some ladies from the area so that we both would have some contacts for future years. The word was out that Goucher College was inviting all Midshipmen to a dance after the game, Plebes included. We were fortunate to meet two lovely ladies soon after our arrival and made a point of dominating their time for the rest of the evening. Thankfully our behavior was at our best and we all got along fine. As the bewitching hour approached, all Plebes were to report back to the buses for the ride back to USNA. One of the ladies intimated that she had a car and if we would stay longer, she would drive us back to the Academy. Well, this was one of those classic moral battles between duty and pleasure. Neither of us was prone to rash decisions, but for some reason, possibly being the mood of the moment, we opted for pleasure. We soon were to realize the foolishness of this decision.

When the dance was finally over, we headed out to the young lady's car and started for Annapolis with plenty of time to spare. She knew a shortcut, so we were full of confidence. We knew we had plenty of time as it was only 2100 and we had two hours to go: Plebes were due in at 2300, third class at 2330, and second class at 2400. Wrong!!!

As might be expected, the lady got totally lost, and finally around 2300 we stopped at an old farmhouse with a dimly lit porch to ask a farmer the way to Annapolis. When he was not very sure of the directions, panic started to rear its ugly head. We both had that uneasy feeling of knowing we had not done the right thing and now we were going to be caught, and suffer those penalties we knew we would deserve. This caused sweaty hands and palpitating hearts, to say the least. Even the sweetness of the two lovely ladies apologizing for our dilemma did not assuage the situation much.

Well, the Gods were with us. The lady driving at last found her way to the main highway, and drove up to the main gate about 2345. A light drizzle had started, so mids coming in at that hour were wearing raingear, which, of course, have no rank insignia. So Dick and I donned our raingear (prescribed to carry to the game by some savior of higher rank), and walked in with the second class just like we belonged.

As we got to our room, our other two roomies, Dick Dodson and Gene Burroughs, were in a panic wondering what had happened to us. They told us to get into the sack quick as the OOD would soon be making his rounds. We both hopped in fully clothed and no sooner had pulled the blankets over us, and in walked the OOD for a bed check. My heart was beating so loudly I was sure he could hear, but, no, he merely passed on his way. We made it unscathed, but definitely a little smarter and wiser.

Bob Osmon '60

XV

Doth the funnels make war with the paint work?

Do the decks to the cannon complain?

Nay, they know that some soap or a scraper

Unites them as brothers again.

Primping

During Plebe Summer I was attached to Charlie Company, Eighth Platoon, Third Squad. The other two platoons in my company were the Seventh and the Ninth, and we all shared the third deck in the Fifth Wing of Bancroft Hall. The wing was divided into three sections by the intrusion of two separate stairways that had doorways on either side of them, making each section of the wing a separate passageway accessible only through the stairwell transom. My room was the only Eighth Platoon room in its passageway; the eleven remaining rooms belonged to Seventh Platoon. So, prior to meals and those times when the upperclassmen held training in platoon areas, my roommates and I were usually out of Seventh Platoon's way and dealing with our own upperclassmen through the stairwell at the other end of the wing. Consequently, I never thought for a moment that Seventh Platoon's activities should concern me as I had my own chain of command to worry about.

For several weeks I overheard their Squad Leaders and Platoon Commander drilling them on rates and professional knowledge. Like Eighth Platoon, the Plebes would stand in the passageway prior to meals doing calisthenics and close-order drill with brooms, mops, and perhaps even mattresses. On this particular day my Squad Leader was satisfied that the twelve Plebes under his command had memorized their requisite knowledge for the day, knew their menus, and had read the paper sufficiently enough to summarize two front-page and one sports-page article. He dismissed us ten minutes early to change our uniforms for evening meal formation, and I found myself chopping back toward Seventh Platoon.

From what I could spy on my way back, Seventh Platoon's activities that evening were fairly standard. Plebes were braced-up against the passageway bulkheads, standing in rigidly exaggerated poses of attention answering questions, doing push ups when they answered incorrectly, and shouting a lot of "yes Sirs!" Nothing really out of the ordinary, so I felt no compunction about chopping by them, as I would not have to pass through their activities to get to my room.

As I stood over my sink, I noticed that things were heating up outside. The upperclassmen were not satisfied with the Plebes' performance. They grew loud and angry, making life harder for their charges, who sounded as if they were having a hard enough time already. Just then the First Squad leader of Seventh Platoon, the same upperclassman who caught my "Go Army" blunder, stormed into the room. He took one look at me standing at the sink in my skivvies and said, "what the hell are you doing in here primping yourself up for formation when your classmates are in trouble out there in the P-way!" By the time I caught my breath he was already gone and back at the throats of thirty or so Seventh Platoon Plebes.

I jumped into my uniform, quickly buffed the brim of my cover and the toes of my shoes with a rag and sprinted out into passageway. My goal was to avoid this Firstie and get over to my platoon area as quickly as possible. Once sighted, however, I was immediately summoned to take station in the center of the passageway between two facing ranks of Seventh Platoon Plebes.

One by one, the Plebes were ordered to chop to the center of the hallway and stand facing me. Once in position, the other Plebe and I raced through our rates as the Squad Leader called them out. The object was to get through the answer as loud and as fast as possible, without mistakes, and beat your opponent.

It began with the menu for evening meal, the menu for morning meal the following day, the General Orders of a Sentry, random verses from the 28-stanza poem *The Laws of the Navy*, the mission of the Naval Academy, bits of trivia about the Academy grounds known as "Yard Gouge," and it went on like that for the next five or six minutes.

One Seventh Platoon Plebe after another was pitted against me. We stood not one foot apart, shouting at the top of our lungs. We went through everything from what kind of ice cream was being served in King Hall that evening to the Code of Conduct. After beating six of his Plebes I was curtly dismissed.

That was the last bit of trouble I received from that Squad leader, at least for that week.

Jeff Conklin '93

The Dimple in the Middle

John Paul Jones had said that a naval officer must be "a capable mariner, a gentleman of liberal education, of refined manner, have punctilious courtesy and the nicest sense of personal honor."

Captain Mile Draemel, Commandant of Midshipmen, had added "his necktie should always have a dimple in the middle."

After the Captain's directive was published, a few recalcitrant Midshipmen were apparently unwilling or unable to put the required dimple in the middle or in fact anywhere else in their neckties. This fact had been recorded and reported to the Commandant on a number of occasions. So what could be done to impress the importance of this proper sartorial custom?

Apparently, more Midshipmen in the 2nd Battalion had failed to put the dimple in the middle than in the rest of the regiment. So, the whole battalion was put on report. And we all marched for an hour of' extra duty as a consequence.

To this day, I still note whether on television or in real life the necktie has a proper dimple in the middle. And, I still check my own necktie, thanks to Captain Draemel.

Bill Patterson '43

Hot Oil Treatment

The hectic school week combined with sports, studies and Midshipman responsibilities offered little time to relax. My closest friend Becky Ingraham and I found a way to soften our hectic schedules with a weekly respite in the basement of 7th wing. The female Midshipmen hair salon was a place we could hide, relax and enjoy the civilian feminine companionship of its two prize possessions, Flo and Pat.

Once a week we would schedule a hot oil treatment which was our chance to be greeted with friendly smiles and literally "let our hair down." Flo and Pat were always jovial and knew each female mid personally. The conversation turned from the weather to the new uniform regs to Pat's camping trips and Flo's church bake-offs. Through the four years our relationship changed from our being nervous Plebes "Yes, Maming" them to death to becoming confident 1/C Midn and Ensigns who sadly departed from the 7th wing basement considering Flo and Pat as friends.

Even though Bancroft Hall has physically changed a lot since 1994 I am sure that any female who has passed through its halls and down its ladders still holds found memories of two of its hidden secrets, Flo and Pat.

Tara Caroselli '94

The Perfect Tuck

Like the dimple in the tie, the Marine Corp."tuck" was a technique to be mastered by all Midshipmen at the Naval Academy. It gave the impression of being squared away, gung-ho, and attentive to one's military bearing and appearance. And, most important of all, it was a mandatory practice. Those who mastered the technique could be virtually assured of passing inspections without a second glance, assuming of course that there were no other obvious discrepancies.

The tuck was accomplished by holding your trousers around your thighs by standing bow-legged, pulling your blouse down straight, then gripping the side seams of the blouse between your middle fingers and the palm of your hand and pulling the shirt tight. Then, using your thumbs to push the excess fabric forward between your waist and the seams, you would pull the seams backward creating a tapered fit. If this isn't hard enough, the trick is to hold the blouse in this tight position while raising your trousers and fastening them.

Because of the degree of difficulty and dexterity required to do it right, these tucks were frequently administered by one's roommate. But should the roommate be otherwise engaged, it was important to know how to self-administer the perfect tuck.

One of our more creative classmates devised a contraption consisting of a number of elastic straps and clamps to ensure a perfect self-administered tuck without the contortions normally required to achieve the desired affect. Because Midshipmen come in all sizes and shapes, this apparatus had to be custom-designed. Not only did it simplify the tuck procedure, but also it allowed a Midshipman to complete the maneuver unassisted by roommates or passers by. It was absolutely ingenious. The world should know about this invention; certainly the Brigade.

But the genius behind the apparatus preferred to keep his anonymity for fear his invention would be viewed as evidence of laziness, or possibly an attempt to circumvent long standing convention. He went on to obtain patents on other inventions, but never for the automated tuck.

Anonymous

XVI

So ye, being Heads of Departments,

Do your growl with a smile on your lip,

Lest ye strive and in anger be parted,

And lessen the might of your ship.

Pulling Through

Midshipmen with failing grades were called before the Academic Board to explain their misfortunes and, if lucky, be awarded the privilege of taking re-exams in the failed subjects. To all that suffered the slings and arrows of these "inquisitions," they became vivid and indelible memoirs. I carried mine throughout my entire life because it taught me a valuable lesson.

If you were a Midshipman during the 1940s and perhaps a few years beyond, failing marks in any subject landed you "in the bush." And if your grades in that subject didn't improve, you found yourself "on the tree," in which case you also found yourself on the restricted list. Bush and tree notices were posted on Company bulletin boards weekly and I can still hear the moaning, groaning and cursing they evoked from hapless Mids, particularly the treed ones, as it meant having to cancel weekend plans with one's "hot new drag," or "o & o."

I became intimately familiar with these syndromes, particularly in Youngster year, when all the privileges denied you as a Plebe were finally restored, making life at the Academy a bit more bearable.

My euphoria was short-lived, however, as I found myself bushed and treed *ad infinitum* and wound up Youngster year bilging (flunking, to the uninitiated) Steam (fluid mechanics), Juice (electricity & electronics), and Ordnance.

I was summoned before the Academic Board along with other flunkees, but none in this hapless group was flunking more than one subject and their chances for being given re-exams seemed a lot brighter than mine.

The Academic Board was headed by Naval Academy Superintendent, Admiral James L. Holloway, Jr. The other members, mostly Captains, were Heads of the Academic Departments. Never had mine eyes beheld a greater concentration of gold braid and ribbons. And behind all that intimidating glitter were stares that could have shrunk a field of violets.

"How come, Laric, that you're doing so well in English, History & Government (a subject affectionately referred to by Midshipmen as "Bull") but failing miserably in three!! (the exclamation points were there, believe me) technical subjects?"

I mumbled a reply, but can't for the life of me remember what I said. It couldn't have been much, for how do you explain failure except to admit it and take your lumps?

"I see from your record, Laric, that you're quite a linguist," said Admiral Holloway. "How did you acquire this ability?"

"I grew up in Yugoslavia and I attended schools there and in other countries, Sir." "Just how many languages do you speak, Laric?" asked one of the Department Heads. "Six, Sir."

"What are they?" the Captain continued.

"Well, Sir, I speak Slovenian, Serbo-Croatian, French, German and Russian, which I studied here."

"But that's only five," said the Captain, counting on his fingers.

"I also speak English, Sir," I uttered in a whisper, while trying to keep a straight face.

With that, Admiral Holloway let go a rollicking belly-laugh and was immediately joined by all except one Board member, whose slightly crimson face nevertheless betrayed a self-deprecating grin.

I was given re-exams by unanimous vote along with Admiral Holloway's admonition to "hit the books and get going." I did just that and, on returning from Summer Cruise, passed all three exams. But the real lesson learned from this experience was that a touch of humor can open many a door - and I've thanked Admiral Holloway for this lesson ever since.

Paul Laric '49

The First Rhodes Scholar

"Midshipman First Class Turner, Mr. Secretary. Welcome to the Naval Academy." It was May 1946 on Worden Field. Secretary of the Navy James V. Forrestal had just reviewed our weekly Wednesday afternoon parade. From under his broad-brimmed fedora, Forrestal barked to me, "Turner, I understand you want to he a Rhodes Scholar." Taken aback, I stumbled out with, "Yes, sir, but the Navy has a regulation against officers competing for Rhodes Scholarships." The course of my life was about to change.

This had all started a few weeks before, when I had arranged an appointment with the Commandant of Midshipmen to ask whether he thought the regulation in question could be changed. About an hour later he called me back to his office, where he introduced me to Mr. Ferdinand Eberstadt, Chairman of the Secretary of the Navy's Board of Visitors to the Naval Academy that year. James Collier, a classmate, came in on my heels. The Commandant then left, saying Mr. Eberstadt wanted to chat privately with a couple of Midshipmen.

It was an uneventful discussion until Mr. Eberstadt said, "Turner, the Commandant tells me you want to be a Rhodes Scholar." "Yes, sir," I replied, "but the Navy has a regulation against it." He assured me he would talk to the "Secretary" about it. I immediately thought he meant the Secretary of the Board of Visitors. But I soon learned that Eberstadt was a long time confidant of James Forrestal.

Out on the parade field, the Secretary turned to the Vice Admiral on his left, Louis E. Denfeld, the Chief of naval personnel. "Louis, I think we ought to change that regulation." The regulation was changed. I competed, won, and went on to Oxford. And the navy has had 25 Rhodes Scholars in the years since – thanks to James V. Forrestal.

Stansfield Turner '47

Editor's Note: Retired Admiral Turner was Director of the Central Intelligence Agency in the Carter administration. He also served as President of the Naval War College and as Commander-in-Chief, Allied Forces Southern Europe.

Eureka

I have two lasting impressions and remembrances of my Academy days. They stand out because they were psychologically and practically so strong and are today as poignant as ever and will remain so.

In May, 1945, as an enlisted man I realized with alarm that I was going to enter the Naval Academy as a Plebe. Anticipating the worst in my Plebe indoctrination, I took solace from my conviction that "they can't kill me." I will never forget the final day of my Fourth Class year when, as an ending gesture, I was made to crawl up on top of my locker until midnight.

In May, 1949, 1 was standing in front of the final, FINAL !! examination grade listing for one of my weakest technical subjects. My eyes quickly ran down the list: "Sprague 2.5." I had DONE IT. I had MASTERED the greatest challenge I could imagine. I had DONE it. It was inconceivable, yet gloriously pride-giving.

David Sprague '49

XVII

Dost think, in a moment of anger,

'Tis well with thy seniors to fight?

They prosper, who burn in the morning,

The letters they wrote over-night.

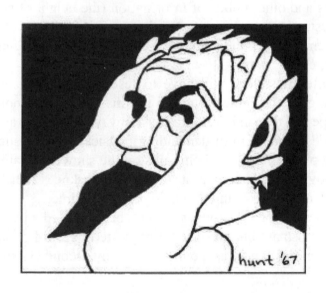

The Come-Around

Perhaps the most enduring of the physically and psychologically challenging traditions at the Naval Academy, the "Come Around" is a command performance of sorts. The subject, the lowly fourth classman know as the Plebe, needs commit a violation no greater than glancing sideways (taking his eyes out of the boat) to be ordered to come around or report to the room of an upper classman for an attitude adjustment session.

This session consists of the Plebe being drilled to demonstrate his rote memorization ability as he recites passages, statistics and historical minutia from his handbook of naval trivia known as *"Reef Points."* These sessions also test his general knowledge of academics, sports, current events and other tidbits of information (the height of Mount Everest, the number of windows panes in the Naval Academy chapel, the number of cobble stones on Tecumseh court, etc.)

Often the Plebe will have to research a subject before arriving for the come around to test his ability to respond to unexpected demands. And almost always, the come around includes some form of demanding physical activity, such as doing 50 pushups, or 25 chin ups on the shower curtain bar, or shoving out (standing at attention with knees half bent) for what seems like interminable periods of time.

These come arounds can be ordered by any upperclassman, but are usually requested by third classmen (sophomores) know as Youngsters, or by second classmen (juniors). There are frequent time conflicts with too many come arounds requested at the same time, which have to be negotiated. The youngsters usually defer to the second classmen, but may in return for giving up their time slot ask for two come arounds at a later date.

These come arounds can also entail a degree of servitude, spit-shining the upper classman's shoes; dismantling, oiling and reassembling their M-1 rifle used in P-rades. And occasionally it includes bringing the upper classmen food or candy (gedunk).

The Plebes may be asked to perform for the upperclassmen, solo dancing to music, taking a shower fully clothed, or singing a song to entertain their superiors.

And many times, on reporting for their come around, the Plebe will be ordered to return to their rooms and change uniforms in an unrealistic interval – 2 minutes. These are called "uniform races." The uniforms are usually standard outfits – dress blues, mess dress, white works, etc., and may require cuff links, studs, leggings over your boots, insignias and appropriate award ribbons – but sometimes the uniform requested is not a standard issue variety (socks, jocks and lockbox)

You can imagine the condition of the Plcbe's room after these uniform changes, there not being time to fold, stow and hang up the uniform he has just changed out of. Needless to say, a Plebe's room should be suitable for inspection at all times.

These come arounds are time consuming, require much physical effort and dexterity, and create a level of mental stress that has no equivalent in the civilian world.

And the come arounds typically take place during the evening when the Plebe could well use the time for academic homework and studying for exams. If there is one thing that the come around teaches a Plebe, it's time management and the ability to prioritize. Because of the scarcity of time, Plebes can often be found in the bathroom inside a toilet stall, studying for the next day's exams after "lights out."

While this character-building activity will, to readers unacquainted with this practice, seem like a sadistic form of torture, most Midshipmen who went through the program will be the first to tell you that it is most beneficial.

The come around is not an event that a Plebe looks forward to. It is a form of discipline that sometimes has not apparent value. Just trying to avoid invitations to come around makes a Plebe very conscious of his actions, very mindful of what errors in judgment, blemishes in uniform or bearing, can result in such a come around. A Plebe becomes aware that he is always being judged – that his every action is subject to criticism and correction.

The memorization sharpens the mind, makes him a quick study, and able to follow commands without having to have those commands be repeated. It makes him a good listener and able to respond to requests that may not always make sense to him at the time because he doesn't have the "big picture" and may not understand the reason for the request.

In war, many times commands need to be given without the luxury of providing an explanation.

The come around, besides being a learning experience for the Plebe, is also a learning experience for the upper classman. The Youngster or second classman gains the experience of giving orders and ensuring that these orders are responded to correctly, in a timely manner, and with the proper attitude on the part of the subordinate. It provides an opportunity to give constructive criticism and set an example of a cool and confident professional to which the Plebes will aspire.

The Plebes also gain the experience of finding out what it's like to succeed in a demanding environment. They learn that, despite their best efforts, there are times when they will fall short of expectations, but will be given another chance to prove themselves worthy.

It is an unreal environment that is thrust upon them. Some will decide for themselves that this is not for them, and willingly tender their resignations. Some will never succeed in fulfilling the expectations for their performance and will be drummed out. But the majority of them will stick it out, knowing that in less than a year, they will be in the position to give come-arounds to the new Plebe class. They will become upper classmen – which is both an honor and a responsibility. They will be expected to demonstrate leadership skills. And they will have done for them what, as a Plebe, they had to do for the upper classmen.

All in all, the come around gives the Plebes an opportunity to prove to themselves and to others their mental and physical toughness and gain the confidence, self esteem and self assurance to continue in the officer training program.

Richard Zino '67

Editor's Note: The come around has changed in nature over the years. Even though the basic intent - to teach forth class Midshipmen mental toughness and provide an opportunity for them to demonstrate their ability to respond quickly to unforeseen circumstances - has remained the same from generation to generation, the come around no longer takes time out of a Plebe's study period. Activities are less servile and more directly keyed to the Midshipman's professional development.

The Linen Cart Races

I suspect the linen cart races were strictly a 14th Company (old style, 24-company Brigade in 1947-8) evolution. My mental picture is of pushing Dick Ambrogi (48-B) down the corridor of the 2nd wing toward the 4th wing, at 2145 (release from quarters) as fast as I could. I believe the firstie in the competing cart might have been his "wife," Bill Langone (48-B). Dick was wearing a gorilla or chimpanzee full rubber mask. He was jumping up and down in the cart like an ape, spinning around as we passed astonished Mids, and shouting: "HOO! HOO! HOO!" while scratching the sides of his ribs.

Ambrogi was a dear fellow who made a joke of everything. I was a scared Plebe, during much of the first half-year, anyway, being an only child whose father died when I was only 12. I was pretty overwhelmed by the dynamism and positivism of all the military stuff and order and discipline and, especially, the contrasts offered by the strong personalities of some of the upperclassmen. Seeing one of the first class taking everything so casually and making fun of sacred cows eased the way for me a lot, and I bet Dick never knew that.

It is pleasant to reminisce now, but shocking to realize the immensity of time that has gone by and even more so to try to make sense out of it all - or even some of it.

Charles D. McIntosh '51

Cruise Box Races

Back in 1945, the Plebes (class of '49) were "invited to participate" in cruise box races. Now a cruise box measures about 30" x 30" x 60" with a hinged top and a hasp to secure its contents. These were issued to Midshipmen near the end of Plebe year. They were placed in the corridor outside the Midshipman's rooms and used to stow uniforms, valuables and other belongings for summer cruises. (Later in their careers, officers use these cruise boxes for shipment of belongings to distant duty stations, TDY or other assignments).

As a Plebe, not much gear had yet been accumulated to fill or even justify having a cruise box. But as Midshipmen advance to the upper classes it sometimes became difficult to fit necessities in this 30 cubic foot container. Being relatively free of clutter, the principle use of a Plebe's container was for what were known as "cruise box races."

This is not what you may think. They were not equipped with wheels, did not slide easily across the corridor floor, and although made of wood, they were not watertight enough to float or be navigated even in reflection pools or oversized puddles.

No, while the cruise box races involved a considerable amount of movement, the cruise boxes themselves remained stationery. And while this was indeed a race, only a single cruise box was needed to conduct the exercise, although frequently two or more were involved in these activities. It worked as follows:

A Plebe – no other class would willingly succumb to such a feat of agility – would show up for a come-around to an upper classman's room, prepared for a session of rigorous activity. In addition to the clothing on his back, the Plebe would bring with him a change of uniform as well. On the command, the Plebe would climb into a nearby cruise box taking the extra (completely different type) uniform with him, including a change of shoes, socks, belt, tie, detachable collar, trousers, blouse and jacket if these were part of the chosen dress. Then the lid of the box would be closed and latched and a dramatic count down would begin: on your mark, get set, go!

The Plebe would then proceed to change clothes within the limited confines of the cruise box without the benefit of light to see by. And all the while he would be trying to set an individual speed record or compete with another unfortunate Plebe for the evening honors.

Of course the upper classmen did not stand idly by. They shouted derogatory comments at their Plebe, "What's taking so long, What are you doing in there, taking a nap?" (Actually they didn't say taking a nap, but this is the clean version) Sometimes they even asked the Plebes to recite navy folklore while going through the Houdini-like contortions needed to make a successful change of attire.

It had been roughly calculated that there was enough oxygen in the cruise box to sustain an average size Plebe for up to ten minutes. But the physical activity combined with the stuffy environment caused a goodly amount of perspiration to accumulate. As might be expected there was much banging and thrashing about. Should there be a noticeable reduction in the noise level normally associated with a cruise box race, the upper classmen would quickly open the lid and allow some fresh air to revive the exhausted Plebe. Many times they would pop the lid just to monitor the progress and provide some words of inspiration.

It was not unusual for the cruise box race to follow immediately after a rigorous round of physical activity such as running up to the 4th deck (6th floor) and back multiple times. This ensured that both sets of clothes were thoroughly sweat-drenched and difficult to change into and/or out of.

Naturally the Plebes who excelled were those who were slight of build, nimble and had a low coefficient of perspiration. Being double-jointed didn't hurt either, but I don't recall any classmates being blessed with this gift.

Tom Seelye '49

Editor's Note: This character-building activity was short lived. Although many have heard about it, few have experienced it, and the tradition of Cruise Box Races apparently vanished from routine use some time in the 1950's

XVIII

For some there be, shelved and forgotten,

With nothing to thank for their fate,

Save that (on a half-sheet of foolscap)

Which a fool "Had the honor to state."

Commence Firing

Our class entered the Academy after V-E Day and before V-J Day of World War II. Most of the class of '49 had prior military service, mostly in the Navy. Some even had commissions. Consequently, we weren't intimidated by the Academy's time honored traditions. There were countless incidents that showed our class's independent spirit and initiative. Many hours were spent by our class standing in formation at attention while we were extorted to "own up" to some mischievous prank. My favorite was the incident of the Saluting Batteries.

One Wednesday afternoon during our Youngster year, after last class but before the weekly parade, John C. (name omitted to protect the not-so-innocent) and I walked by the saluting battery overlooking the Severn River, on our way to Bancroft hall. We noticed that sailors and marines were unloading ammunition that was to be used to render honors to the Secretary of the Navy when he arrived on Academy grounds.

John made a quick note of the call box located near the battery. The guards at the main gate would alert the crew of the saluting battery when to fire the honorary salute. John and I ran back to Bancroft hall. He went into the Battalion Commander's office that was unoccupied, picked up the phone, dialed the saluting battery's telephone number and stated in a loud and authoritative voice, "Stand By, Commence Firing."

169

We ran to our rooms, laughing almost hysterically after we heard the first of the saluting battery's volley. Boom. Boom. Boom. Boom. Boom. Boom. Six salvos were fired before there was silence. The Secretary of the Navy never received his salute of 19 guns. Sufficient ammunition hadn't been broken out of the armory to fire 25 rounds.

That night the Class of '49 stood at attention for over an hour while our company officers waited fruitlessly for the "guilty" party to confess.

The Class of '49 had struck again.

Al Levine '49

Ringing the 'Enterprise' Bell

I remember that Hal Hall, who lived at the Tecumseh end of the 2nd wing, swabo deck with later-to-be Admiral Bryan Compton, played a good trick on the fearsome Lt. DeLargy, known for handing out fraps faster than a speeding bullet.

Hal ducked out after dark and tied a long black thread to the clapper of the *Enterprise* bell which was located, as a of commemorative wartime monument, to the right of the steps as you face Bancroft Hall. He led the thread back through his end window, then sneaked around to the side of the building and back into his room. Just after taps at 2200, he went to his window, pulled gently on the thread then eased off, then kept repeating this action.

By continuing to tug at the thread, then letting go, as the clapper reached the end of its swing, he got the clapper swinging more and more. At last, it touched the bronze dome softly, and a whisper of a "gong" could be heard.

Another tug, the release, and a slightly louder "gong" sounded. Some of us woke up.

There was still no reaction from the Main Office, so Hal kept tugging. "Gong," "Gong," "Gong," and finally a thunderous "GONG !!!"

That did it. There was a clatter from the Main Office that echoed across the courtyard, as DeLargy slammed his chair forward and grabbed for his sword - ready to do battle.

"MESSENGER-R-R!" we heard him yell. This was followed by the sound of two sets of running footsteps down the front steps of Bancroft Hall. The "we" who heard all this were now probably several hundred wide-awake Mids.

"GONG !!!"

171

By now, the enraged OOD and his Plebe messenger had passed the "CLR" brick, and were halfway to the offending bell of the long-dead carrier *Enterprise*. But surely it was no ghostly crewman from the depths who was tolling ...was it?

"GONG !!!"

With this one last ringing insult, just as the frustrated, boiling officer and his hapless messenger reached the bell, Hal yanked the thread, which broke at the clapper. He hauled in the only physical evidence of a human agency.

The ringing stopped, but all over the section of Bancroft Hall that faced the front courtyard there were stifled giggles. Whether Lt. DeLargy heard those or not isn't known, of course. But it is likely that he long remembered the spectral ringing of that bell.

The bell had been placed in its prominent position by the Superintendent, VAdm. Harry Hill. It was intended, he said at its dedication, to elevate the morale and team spirit of the Brigade of Midshipmen.

It worked - at least once, anyway. Morale was never higher than on the night the *Enterprise* bell rang, all by itself.

Charles D. McIntosh '51

For Whom the Bell Tolls

In the latter half of my Plebe year, I and several of my classmates were rustled from our sleep late one Friday night by two of our company's more "playful" Youngsters. It was clear from their breath that they had been imbibing -- what and how much was not clear, but they were undoubtedly under the influence. They told us that we had been chosen to join them in a run to the top of the Mahan Hall tower. Not wishing to risk their wrath if we were to decline, we accepted their call to honor, such as it was.

The Youngsters then led us from our rooms on 4-0 into the cellars of Bancroft and into the heating ducts which run the length of Stribling Walk from Mahan to Bancroft. For the life of us, we had not known these ducts existed. Although lighted, this tunnel was dim and musty and less than inviting. Our flashlights provided us little comfort from what lay not only ahead, but all around us. The large steam pipes were, as one might expect, fairly hot and provided each of us with burns we were to remember for quite some time. As we approached Mahan from our subterranean tunnel, we took a sharp right and emerged in the yard immediately outside Sampson Hall.

Doing our best John Belushi impersonation (see Animal House), we scooted around behind Mahan. Jumping on the shoulders of the taller Youngster, one of my classmates grabbed hold of the lower, spring-action ladder of the fire escape at the rear of the Hall. We quickly scampered up the escape to its apex, at which we found an unlocked door leading to the walkway around the base of the Mahan tower dome. A narrow staircase, spiraling as I recall it, led up to the bell tower itself. Moving quickly, we soon found ourselves looking down from the tower out over the yard. We had made it, without alarming (or awakening, as the case may be) a single jimmylegs, the civilian guards then contracted to patrol the grounds.

At that moment of triumph, which I am sure may only be matched by scaling Everest or K-2, our exhilaration was shattered when one of the Youngsters began hammering the large bell with a two-by-four he had found on the deck. The tolling of the bell (and we as Plebes knew enough not to ask for whom it tolled ... it tolled for WE!) was loud enough to awaken jimmylegs all over the yard. The police lights were activated on their vehicles as they quickly converged Mahan. No matter what we did, we could not tear the Youngster away from his incessant clanging. Time was running out, the jimmylegs would have the tower surrounded in a matter of minutes and we would be "fried. " The bell-ringer yelled at us to go -- apparently he thought he could "cover us."

We sprinted from the tower, taking the narrow steps leading down to the base of the dome in threes. If any one of us were to fall, we would all be doomed. We successfully negotiated the narrow stairs and made our way to the fire escape. The first of us took the spring action ladder in full stride and each of us followed in turn as the ladder streaked downward. It hit the ground with a deafening clang and sprang upward again, catapulting the lead man 15 feet through the air. The rest of us held on for dear life until the ladder settled on the ground. By this time, the jimmylegs cars could be heard racing from all reaches of the yard, their sirens pitched against the Annapolis night and the continued clanging of the bell. It was clear that at least some of the jimmylegs had us in their sights. We raced around the hall and dove, some of us headfirst, some feet first, into the exhaust duct outside Sampson. We could hear the jimmylegs, now on foot, hoofing it around the corner of Sampson. Thankfully, no one had seen us dive into the duct and we were not going to wait around to see if they could find us. We blindly sprinted back down the steam pipe path toward ole' Mother B. That none of us were lost or killed in that mad dash is one the true miracles of our time. We made it back to our rooms, sweating, chests heaving, utterly terrified and still, amazingly, listening to the Youngster tolling away on the Mahan Tower bell.

We awoke the next morning to find the Youngster sound asleep in his room. For some reason, the jimmylegs never scaled the tower in search of our modern-day Quasimodo, and, after waiting an appropriate amount of time, he calmly descended from his perch.

Whether any of this contributed to the building of my character or to my development as a leader is of course suspect. Nevertheless, it is forever etched and cherished in my memory of my four years on the shores of the Severn.

Rich Hans '83

Snippets from the Class of '62

During Plebe year the second class in our company challenged us to a snowball fight. On the day of the fight positioned themselves on the third deck and we were in the courtyard...and we got to bring them fresh snowballs when they ran out.

Phone booth stuffing was the intercollegiate rage in the late '50's. Our showers were just about that size! The 2/c supervised the stuffing of 17 Plebes and were trying for another when a guy on the bottom next to me broke wind. Abandon ship drill went into effect immediately with the 2/c being nearly trampled.

One of my classmates first class year made an official suggestion that we have Air Raid Drills - just what we needed-another drill! He spent the next two months in a constant stage of readiness in the mess hall - Plebes from all over the brigade were sent, arms outstretched and making airplane noises, to dive bomb our hero. Some or the bombs were butter, some jelly, some milk.

We did the Great Lakes Cruise as youngsters. On duty days we wore White Works and guided hundreds of tourists about the ship. The visitors were met at the brow personnel on watch and we quickly noted that the prettiest girls avoided the Mids. We learned later that the brow greeters were telling the lovelies to avoid the fellows with blue rings on their hats as they had social diseases!

Remember the first Air Force Game in Baltimore? Their falcon mascot flew to the HAMM's Beer sign on the scoreboard and stayed there for the whole game. The falconers didn't know of the Mid with the ultrasonic transmitter who was seated with the brigade.

Two of us were on a come-around and were "hunkered" (at a brace of course) on top of the old metal room lockers. The door banged open and the O.D charged in. He was that short, chubby fellow known as TF (Too Fat to Fly). He knew there were Plebes in the room - he just never looked up!

The 2/c would put two of the old desks together. My short roommate would put some polish on the desks, place a towel over the wax and sit on the towel. We had to put his legs straight out and I had to grab the legs and do laps around the desk - Great Buffer!

The 2/c had us around to do push-ups (our class number plus one = 63). A marine Major was O.D. that night and he came slamming into the room. I had the satisfying thought that two second-classmen were about to seriously fried. Instead, he looked down at me being in the push-up position, and told me "GET LOWER ON YOUR NEXT PUSH-UP MISTER! Plebe Year was not always a fair time!

Vic Reiling '62

177

XIX

Dost deem that thy vessel needs gilding,

And the dockyard forbear to supply;

Place thy hand in thy pocket and gild her,

There be those who have risen thereby.

The Hop

Christmas formal dance 1960! Youngster year going very nicely. Here I was with my date at the formal Christmas dance. During the 60's no one was allowed to leave the dance early (except first classmen). Each class had specific times to be back in the safety of Mother Bancroft and for a youngster that was within 45 minutes of the completion of the dance.

To maximize one's time at the drag house, my date and I were dancing on the upper level of Dahlgren close to where our coats and hats were located. Every short cut was utilized to minimize the time between end of *Navy Blue and Gold* and the mad dash to the drag house.

As we were snuggling close to the smooth flow of *"Good Night Irene,"* I suddenly felt a tap on my shoulder. I couldn't believe that someone was cutting in on me! It was the last dance! When I turned to tell the individual what I thought of this exceedingly bad display of tact, I found myself staring at a fourth classman from my company who was the Mate of the Watch with the OOD. I got fried for "Public Display of Affection - Dancing too Close;" 15 demerits and three hours of early morning calisthenics to reflect on my immoral behavior. Who says there isn't a Santa Claus??!

Peter D. Quinton '63

Tea Fights

Back in 1963 a Plebe's only hope of a brief encounter with the opposite sex was during Saturday afternoon "Tea Dances" in Dahlgren Hall sponsored by the Academy. Mrs. Marshall, the social director for many, many years, would arrange for young women to be bussed in from colleges and schools in the area – Goucher, Hood, Wilson, University of Maryland and many others.

They would spend an afternoon meeting Midshipmen and providing an opportunity for all of us to demonstrate our dancing and other social skills. The music would usually be supplied by the Chiefs' Band and the entire event would last about three hours.

Plebes would congregate on the North side of the floor and the young ladies would arrive through the West entrance, and make their way down the wide staircase. Each gender group would pass through a funnel of sorts, one individual at a time. As each woman exited the mouth of the funnel from the steps, a Midshipman would be released. They would pair off and join for their first dance of the afternoon.

The women came in all shapes and sizes. This was their opportunity to meet a Mid and perhaps begin a lasting relationship. If the match was a good one, the couple might stay together for the entire afternoon. Otherwise there would be quite a bit of changing dance partners.

As each Plebe approached the neck of the funnel he would spy his likely partner, and if the girl in the corresponding neck of the distaff funnel was a "catch," all was right with the world. On the other hand, if the probable partner looked like a "brick" (unattractive, without redeeming qualities) the Mid would push backwards in the queue to await a more suitable "date."

As you can imagine, there was quite a bit of shoving and jockeying for position. But when all was said and done, you didn't want to cause a scene and embarrass the young lady, so you would graciously accept the inevitable pairing and dance at least one dance with her, even if she was not Miss America.

I remember doing a bit of jockeying myself, always looking for just the right gal, one who was shorter than me. (I was somewhat vertically-challenged, and very self conscious about it). It could get a bit nasty in the neck of the funnel, and I suspect the women were eyeing us in a similar fashion and doing their own jockeying for position. Thus the name "Tea Fight."

Over the course of six Tea Fights I remember three of the young ladies in particular. One of my early dance partners was Katherine I. Means from Gibson Island not far from the Naval Academy. She called herself Kim. Another was Becky Terrell, a very smart gal who went on to Syracuse University. I traveled up to Syracuse one weekend when our respective football teams were meeting in S-U's stadium, and spent the day with Becky.

But the girl I remember the most was Alice Ratchford from Baltimore. Alice was as cute as a button. I remember doing my fair share of jockeying, timing my arrival at the neck of the funnel just right to be paired off with Alice. She was petite, had a pretty face, and was full of life.

We danced the full three hours together, exchanged mailing addresses and phone numbers, and agreed to meet at a future date. In fact I invited Alice to the Army-Navy game that year in Philadelphia. This was the year that John F. Kennedy was assassinated and the A/N game was delayed one week to allow sufficient time for the country to mourn. Not only did Alice come to the game, but we set up a close friend of hers, Cricket Smith, to be a blind date for my roommate Dick Raaz. Cricket subsequently married another classmate Bill Carver. But I digress.

Alice and I had a great time at the game. Navy won, of course. Roger Staubach was quarterback and we prevailed in the last five seconds of the game, as I recall.

After the game and the many parties had ended, I invited Alice to ride back down to the Academy in the Midshipman busses. We sat up front, right behind the driver – she by the window, I was on the aisle.

As we rode back we talked at length. She told me that her older sister was engaged to a second classman at the Academy. I moved closer. Her family was crazy about the Baltimore Orioles. I put my arm around her. For all of Alice's effervescence and good looks, I was bothered that she seemed a little inhibited when it came to "cuddling." There was something wrong with this picture, but I couldn't put my finger on it. So I confronted her. I needed to know the reason.

I knew Alice was young and hadn't dated a lot. And while I was a bit disappointed that she wasn't yet 18 years old, I was a patient person. I was only 19 myself. But after more probing it turned out that she had lied about her age. She wasn't yet 17. In fact she was barely 16. I felt betrayed. How could she do this to me? We rode the rest of the way home in virtual silence.

Although I did see Alice after that day – she was a good looker and a guy needed companionship – it was never quite the same after that. Alice subsequently dated another Plebe the following year.

Almost 20 years later I was a civilian and attending a technology seminar in Boston. During a break I struck up a conversation with another attendee from Baltimore. I asked him if he happened to know an Alice Ratchford. He responded affirmatively, said she was married with three children, was very happy, and still a fan of the Orioles.

To this day I still fault Mrs. Marshall for not screening the young ladies who attended the Tea Fights to ensure they were "of age."

Richard Zino '67

Third Wing

About three weeks into Plebe Summer, I was getting the hang of keeping my White Works uniform in check between chow calls and the long, arduous chop from the Fifth Wing of Bancroft Hall to Tecumseh Court for formations. Several of my classmates attended the Naval Academy Prep School and knew a few tricks to square-away the black neckerchiefs we wore with our uniforms Plebe Summer. The best way, they said, to get a neckerchief looking right was to fold it diagonally into a triangle, place a nickel on the two corners opposite the fold, roll it up tightly and secure it with a small piece of scotch tape. The result was a tightly rolled neckerchief that did not loosen over time, allowing you to tie it into a sharp looking square knot. If done properly, the tie hung loosely about your neck in the center of your chest, covering the bottom of your jumper's V-neck. The nickel gave you the right diameter and the tape allowed you to use the neckerchief over and over again without having to roll it up and tie it each time.

With a proper knot and shiny shoes it was relatively easy to avoid negative attention from the upperclass about uniform appearance. This method of preparing the neckerchief was sound with one exception, you could not move around too much because once the knot was tied and centered on your chest, the nickel wound up wrapped in the roll somewhere over your right shoulder. When you chopped down the passageway in that exaggerated, high-stepping, run-almost-in-place run that all Plebes do, the nickel obeyed the law of gravity. It inched its way down to the center of your chest, pulling the neckerchief around with it, leaving the knot on your left shoulder after only a few steps. So, after chopping down four flights of stairs to Tecumseh Court for formation, you were guaranteed to have a wayward knot and a problem if an upperclassman took issue with your present state of disarray. The only way to fix the tie prior to formation where it was strictly forbidden, was to find a classmate's room close to Tecumseh Court. Once sighted, you could duck into the room, fix your neckerchief and screw on your cover which, after four flights had no doubt fallen down over your eyes. After that you could run out to formation.

I became fairly skilled at performing this maneuver and avoided some of the attention other nickel-clad neckerchief wearers suffered from the traveling knots. Or so I thought. One day, when my cover was so far down over my forehead that I saw nothing save my own miserable chopping feet and my neckerchief was in its usual place on my shoulder, I leaned back and sighted an open door from underneath my fallen brim. An open door was a sure sign that the room belonged to a fellow Plebe, a sympathetic comrade. I made my turn, yelled "Go Navy Sir," and found myself staring at two gleaming pairs of white shoes protruding from the legs of two stiffly-starched pairs of trouser legs.

Now, I had only been a Plebe for a couple of weeks, but I still could not remember seeing any classmates of mine wearing white shoes. The uniform Plebes wore to formation called White Works "Charlie." This uniform consisted of pajama-like white cotton jumpers and slacks which tied at the waist, black oxford shoes, a black neckerchief, and a Midshipman cover vice the Plebe "dixie cup." Only upperclassmen wore white shoes, and they wore them with Summer Whites. Spying this discrepancy out from under my tilted brim, I started to remind my classmates that they wearing the wrong shoes and only had two minutes to change them. As I did so, I froze in sudden panic and disbelief. Upon lifting my cover I realized with a rapidly sinking stomach that my comments were unnecessary. I had not, as I originally intended, chopped into a Plebe room. On the far side of the room stood two Three Stripers putting on their swords. When I entered, they turned from looking out the window at the Plebes moving into formation and stared at me, in fact it felt as if they were looking right through me and my crooked neckerchief. All this happening with only two minutes until formation.

I averted their gaze, blurted out "Excuse me, Sir!" and attempted an about-face to get away. The Firstie to my right gave a quick order to halt and about-face, and I wound up back in the center of the room, smack in the middle of these two upperclassmen. They made the standard inquiry "just what do you think you are doing!" I responded in a very nervous tone that my neckerchief knot was coming loose, was not centered on my chest, and that I mistakenly thought this room belonged to a fellow classmate. He walked over to me and in a cold, serious silence inspected my uniform from the peak of my cover to the very tips of my shoes. Then it happened, he quickly straightened my neckerchief, gave the knot a tug to tighten it and told me with a laugh that I had better get going. In disbelief I excused myself and ran. That was the single greatest act of charity I received as a Plebe, although it could have been that neither of them could be late to formation either.

Jeff Conklin '93

XX

If the fairway be crowded with shipping

Beating homeward the harbour to win,

It is meet that, lest any should suffer,

The steamers pass cautiously in.

A Sunburn to Remember

It was the summer of 1940. Our class was on a summer battleship cruise in the Caribbean. We had been working day and night, but the 4th of July was a holiday. So we were anchored off the island of St. Thomas. An inviting white-sand beach beckoned from the shore.

We were given liberty to hit the beach. However, the Midshipmen's officer gently reminded us to avoid too much sun, adding that any Midshipman who became a sunburn case would be put on report.

I remember I did get badly sunburned, but I suffered in silence. I thought I could just sleep it off. Unfortunately, I had hammock-stowing duty next morning. This involved climbing into the hammock nettings to catch hammocks which other classmates would toss up to me.

I remember feeling very cold and sweaty as I prepared to receive the first hammock. But that is all I remember. Waking up in sickbay, I knew I was in trouble. Before long the Midshipmen's officer arrived. I held my breath as he asked the doctor to confirm that I had a bad case of sunburn so he could officially put me on report. The doctor considered the Midshipmen's officer's question carefully. Then, apparently deciding I already was suffering enough, the doctor answered, "No Sir. This Midshipman has a bad case of constipation!"

Bill Patterson '43

Cruise Capers

Today, a half century later, I still recall with much amusement two happenings on Youngster Cruise. We had a wonderful itinerary that included England, Scotland and the Scandinavian countries.

In Edinburgh, if memory serves, the St. Andrews Golf and Tennis Club sent invitations to our ship, the aircraft carrier *Randolph*, for any Midshipmen interested in a tennis challenge on the club's clay courts. A bunch of us immediately volunteered guessing correctly that along with tennis, the club members will surely also treat us to snacks and refreshments that were bound to surpass the *Randolph's* chow line offerings.

Each one of us was to play a match against two of the club's stalwarts. My initial opponent was a middle-aged gentleman with a sure-fire backhand and it took all of my skills and concentration to keep up with him. It was touch and go all the way until, after some dozen sets, I prevailed, but just barely. We shook hands, he congratulated me and said to stand by for my next challenger. I stood by and stood by, tossed a few balls in the air, waited and waited. I suddenly realized that I was the only person left at the tennis courts and there was no sign of my next challenger. So, I parked my racquet, tennis balls and sweater at the gate and made for the Clubhouse. Once inside, I asked about my designated opponent. The kindly gentleman at the desk responded with a whimsical smile, "Don't you Americans know that when it's tea time, everything stops; your partner will be along in due course. Meanwhile, why not join us in a spot of tea?" How could I turn down an age-old tradition?

My next indelible recollection from that cruise took place in beautiful Goteborg, Sweden. I can still see the teeming harbor with its multitude of pleasure craft of every description bobbing up and down in the choppy waters. It was summertime and we were all eager to see the sights and particularly the sandy beaches on the islands outside of Goteborg harbor. Our enthusiasm reached an all-time high on our very first liberty.

My friends and I decided to first hit the beaches and then return to town for a bit of sightseeing and dinner. Some kindly boat people in the harbor asked us to come aboard as they will gladly take us to one of the islands. What luck! The boat ride took only a few minutes and we thanked our hosts and bid them good-bye when we landed at the beautiful little island. A sandy beach, full of bathers and sun worshipers stretched out before us. As we approached, we couldn't believe our eyes. Those beautiful blond Swedish sun-bathers were stark naked. We quickly decided that, "When in Rome, do as the Romans." And so we did.

A couple of days later, word went out that a prominent Goteborg family wanted to treat some Mids to a picnic and a swim at their private home. My friends and I knew better than to pass up an opportunity of good food and good times and we volunteered without hesitation. We were chauffeured to a lovely villa, introduced to the other guests, including some lovely girls, and treated to a lavish spread of Swedish "Smorgasbord."

"How about a swim in the pool?" asked our host. We obliged willingly and, thinking "When in Rome ...," jumped in the water in our birthday suits, unaware of our hosts' and their guests' raised eyebrows, not to mention blushing cheeks of the Swedish lovelies.

When other bathers appeared in their bathing suits, we realized our faux pas and quickly put ours on – to our host's and the ladies' great relief. Later, on our way back to the *Randolph*, we couldn't stop laughing and, once aboard, regaled our friends with this unforgettable Goteborg adventure.

Wesley Brown '49

Sorrowful Episodes

Not all recollections are amusing. We recall the joys but also the sorrows.

It was about a month before our graduation when, upon return from class, we found a Marine Corps major in the room with a classmate who was packing his belongings preparatory to leaving. The major was there presumably to insure that no conversation would occur, perhaps that contagion would not occur. The reason for the peremptory dismissal? The classmate was gay and his homosexuality had been discovered. We were saddened, not only by what was occurring, but also by how the expulsion was stage-managed. It suggested criminality. The crime? A minority sexual orientation.

The first black Midshipman to graduate from the Naval Academy was our own Wesley A. Brown. I had heard stories of others who had tried, come close, only to be thrown out or so hounded that they resigned. I don't know the truth of these stories. I believe that the terrible history should be documented rather than ignored. It is one way to insure that that kind of outrage does not recur. I'm sure Wesley Brown has a lot of stories to tell. I can well understand should he decide to remain silent. But I would be particularly interested in learning of attitudes and actions which reflected credit and encouraged him.

While I was at the Academy, the only Hispanic Midshipmen I ever saw were those appointed from South-American or Central-American countries.

Acceptance of females into the Academies was a milestone. I remember when I was an enlisted man the insulting remarks made about servicewomen. The relatively recent introduction of females into VMI and The Citadel demonstrates continuing gender biases.

All of us are minorities in one way or another, and not only as Blacks, Hispanics, females, foreign-born (or the children of parents who were), Protestants, Roman or Eastern Orthodox, Catholics, Jews, Muslims, Atheists, or Agnostics. History makes it clear that both we as individuals and the composite called our country are better off when such distinctions as gender, color, national origin, religion, or sexual orientation, that are globally unrelated to competencies demanded of applicants or incumbents, play no role in decisions regarding selection or advancement.

Elliott Schuman '49

Editor's Note: Elliott Schuman was, in 1972, the head of a union consisting of faculty members in a private university that concluded the very first collective bargaining agreement with a university administration. As chief negotiator that same year, he was also responsible for personally introducing into the nondiscrimination clause that had been previously employed in most labor-management contracts the phrase "sexual orientation," the first time it was employed anywhere.

XXI

So thou, when thou nearest promotion,

And the peak that is gilded is nigh,

Give heed to thy words and thine actions,

Lest others be wearied thereby.

Grease

The Naval Academy used a system to measure Midshipmen on many aspects of their training to evaluate their aptitude for the Service and ascertain their fitness to be leaders. The process attempted to quantify the evaluations of both superiors and peers in order to facilitate the ranking of Midshipmen under a "Whole Man Concept."

The objective of this exercise was to identify members of the class with the greatest military aptitude, to be assigned positions of leadership in the Brigade. In addition, it identified those members of the class with the least military aptitude, to be given supplemental instruction and possibly, in more extreme cases, to be evaluated (by boards of officers in the executive department) for separation from the Brigade.

Each year Midshipmen were asked to rate other classmates within their company with respect to leadership potential and to rank them from top to bottom according to their military knowledge, skills, bearing, people skills, etc. (from whom would you most want to take orders). We viewed it as a popularity contest.

When all input was collected, massaged, weighted, and cranked through time-tested algorithms, the procedure resulted in a stack ranking. We called this the "Grease" factor. The Midshipmen with the most grease were at the top of the list. And the Midshipmen with the highest position in the stack would be considered for Midshipman officer positions.

Each company had its own command structure – Company Commander (a three-striper), Company Subcommander (two-striper), and Mustering Petty Officer – and these changed each set. There were three sets per academic year – fall, winter and spring – and there were 36 companies.

Above the Company level there was the Battalion command structure with six Battalions, a Regiment command structure (two Regiments) and, lastly, the Brigade command structure. There was much room to exercise leadership if a Midshipman was smart, ship-shape and popular.

The Mids at the top of the list each year tended to stay near the top in succeeding years, so there were a large number of us who never exercised command leadership. There was little opportunity to make quantum advances in the stack ranking unless of course you underwent a personality transplant, suddenly became a genius, or worked your buns off brown-nosing your way past other classmates.

Many of us resigned ourselves to being "also-rans." I must say, very seriously, that during the mid 1960s, those Midshipmen who found themselves in the Company, Battalion, Regiment or Brigade command structure were truly outstanding individuals with few if any shortcomings. They could be counted upon to represent the Academy and the Brigade of Midshipmen with wisdom, polish and poise, and had many loyal supporters among their peers.

There were no "sour grapes" involved. Somehow, despite the popularity aspect of the grease system, it succeeded in identifying the *crème de la crème* of an outstanding group of young people.

I never made striper at any level, but I was in good company with many others in the same boat. Although I never made it to the top of the "grease ladder," I worked hard, got decent grades, and kept my nose clean. Some guys just have the gift and others do not.

To earn a position in the command structure I think you have to have extremely high self-esteem, be gregarious, and make your leadership aspirations known to your peers and your seniors alike. Then you've got to work hard to talk the talk and walk the walk.

Anonymous

Editor"s Note: Over the years the "grease" system has been modified many times, with varying degrees of effectiveness. Its emphases and its methods of stack ranking Midshipmen have changed and these changes significantly altered the way the process was perceived by those being measured. During the 1980s, some grads remember classmates earning grease points by reporting minor infractions on the part of their peers. In effect, they advanced by "dropping a dime" on fellow Mids. This did little to foster support for the process and, for a period of time, undermined the respect that the Brigade of Midshipmen had for its own command structure.

How to Become a Four-Striper
Without Hardly Trying

Now that I am far beyond the reach of the law of the Form-2 and the Executive Department, it is perhaps time for honest confessions of sins.

My naval career started off with a bang. Indeed, the first day of Plebe Summer Tully Shelley, Charlie Styer and I were put on report for talking on a ladder in Bancroft Hall. From there on in, it was all downhill.

As luck would have it, and I had precious little of it at times, I was also put on report the first day of First Class Year, for breaking taps restriction. It was a poignant moment in my life. Betty Carney had been my Best Girl ever since her father, then Commander Robert B. Carney, had greeted me at the door of their home in Georgetown by going to his closet, pulling out a shot gun, and with great ceremony, checking the barrels... without saying a word of greeting. This particular ceremony was punctuated by excited barks and yelps of the Carney's setter, a dog of absolutely no merit whatsoever as a house pet, but who was a devoted and sincere hunter of anything that could be shot in the field. Whenever the dog saw a gun, he would come to life and gyrate furiously.

It happened that Betty's father had been ordered to be the Executive Officer of *California* on the West Coast, which meant that we would be parted for (we thought) a whole year.

Hence, the "good-byes" were taking a little more time than the clocks in Bancroft Hall had provided for the occasion, and we got caught by Lieutenant Lindsay Williamson, the DO, in Smoke Park. Ah well, you can't beat the system.

But actually you can. I was sort of Exhibit A.

Academically, my Plebe and Youngster year, were marked by such a low standing, that I was a shoe-in for what we used to call "The Number Jumping Prize" awarded annually by the Military Order of the World Wars to that Midshipman who showed the greatest improvement in his marks for the second half of the course compared to the first half.

My basic problem was a total lack of application combined with a tremendous aptitude to get into trouble. Actually, although I was only 14 days beyond my 17th birthday when I entered the Academy, I could already boast that I had been five years in high school, and still hadn't graduated. Rooming with Tully Shelley and Charlie Styer didn't help at all. Among the three of us we could not muster sufficient academic skill to impress a kindergarten teacher.

This problem was exacerbated by a standing feud between the Class of 1940, Seventh Company, and the Class of 1941, Seventh Company. We would emerge into the corridors after release from study hall, and play all sorts of games involving swinging our brooms at each other.

The upshot of this was a short-lived policy to assign First Classmen to different battalions than they had served in previously.

One night, the Second Classmen were called to the basement to be told that the feuding simply had to stop. While they were there, Tully, Charlie and I collected all the toilet paper we could find, and festooned the overhead light in a four-man room on Sunshine Alley with the finest May Pole display one could ever hope to find. After the Second Classmen came from the basement, we Youngsters were called down for the same lecture. When we returned to our room, we found our lockers in the middle of the deck, with our bunks on top, and our chairs jammed between the mattresses and the overhead.

Luck being the name of the game, the Duty Officer that night was Uncle Charlie Kirkpatrick, then a Lieutenant and destined to become Superintendent. He was well qualified, because we taught him so much.

Uncle Charlie came along the Sunshine Alley corridor and saw the mounds of toilet paper that had been thrown out the door of the Second Class room! The Second Classmen, of course, had no idea who would perpetrate such an indignity in the hallowed halls of Mother Bancroft.

What Charlie, Tully and I didn't know was that, while we were trying to unengineer the locker-bed-chair system, a rather nasty sign, printed on a green desk blotter, had been tacked on our door proclaiming that we were something or other of a rather anti-social group.

Uncle Charlie saw this; knocked and entered our room ... and the upshot was the (then) very unusual "breaking up" of a room. Charlie and I were unsat in Math, so we were left to dig ourselves out of that problem, and Tully was transferred to the First Battalion. All three of us hit the report for snickering at a threat to cut off the toilet paper supply if we did the festooning bit again.

Now, it turned out, my "Aptitude for the Service" marks closely paralleled my aptitude for getting into trouble with the Executive Department....in inverse proportion. By the end of Youngster Year, I had the inside track on being one rank below Mustering Petty Officer, which was the lowest rank we had for First Classmen.

Second Class Year was somewhat different. Academically, we were into Seamanship, Navigation, Ordnance and Gunnery, and I was smart enough to know that these were the basis for my "profession" (a conviction I did not share *vis-a-vis* differential equations, Molier Diagrams, and chemical formulas with all sorts of transient valences.)

It also turned out that one of the First Class Battalion Commanders had a very weak voice, which tended to crack at Dress P-Rades, much to the embarrassment of the Powers-That-Be. It is amazing what one Midshipman's weak voice can do for another Midshipman's "Aptitude for the Service." The formula is very simple.

First, one must find an embarrassed Executive Department. That was easy, since the vast majority of the Regiment of Midshipmen was dedicated to this particular cause.

Second, one must find a Midshipman with a loud, unmodulated voice, who could be heard from hell and gone. That turned out to be me. Every time I tried to whisper a confidence to a drag, it disturbed the whole neighborhood. I had no secrets, once I opened my mouth.

Third, one needs to combine these factors into a Sound Military Decision, such as a determination to insure that during June Week, when the Second Class was in charge of formations, no weak voices would be tolerated in those whose job was to bark commands.

Fourth, one must start to change the Executive Department Officers by assigning the newly reporting officers to formulate the organization for the Summer Practice Cruise, which, in those happy days, involved embarkation of the new Third Class and the new First Class in three battleships.

And so it came to pass that the newly reporting officers saw my name as the Third Battalion Commander for June Week, and made the assumption that I had earned this position because of high aptitude marks, instead of a strong, unmodulated voice.

Following the assumption, I was assigned as the Midshipman-in-Charge to the Embarkation Detail for *USS Texas*, the Squadron Flagship.

The difficulty here was that my heart was not in it. Indeed, my heart was with Betty Carney, as was almost every element of my conniving mind.

The other element bailed me out. I simply approached five of my classmates in whom I had great faith and confidence, and asked them if they would help me on the Embarkation Detail by taking charge of each of the five "Divisions" in the cruise organization.

I then dismissed the problem from my mind and, as already recorded, got fried the night before the cruise for being in Smoke Park only a few quarters of a few hours after taps.

At reveille the next morning, I awoke with what might delicately be termed a "revolving stomach." I felt awful; my heart was heavy; and being on report was really the least of my worries, else I would have long since been sent to St. Elizabeth's Hospital as a hopeless case.

I was just able to lug my sea bag down to the sea wall and dump it into the motor launch. The trip out to the Annapolis Roads was sheer, unadulterated agony. On arriving at *Texas*, I left my sea bag in the motor launch and headed for the head.

In *Texas*, the head was a marvelous institution. It consisted of a long trough through which sea water was constantly pumped. The seats were positioned over the trough, and it was definitely conducive to side-by-side companionship. It was also conducive to some diabolical turn of the young American mind, for often, the sitter "upstream" would crumple a piece of newspaper, light it with a match, and let it float downstream.

However, on this particular morning, I was in no mood to play "fireship," albeit I was smart enough to get the upstream seat.

While contemplating my grim prospects of not seeing Betty for a year, the Boatswain's pipe sounded down the hatch: "Midshipman Taussig, Report to the Admiral's cabin."

Hell's Bells! I realized that I had broken Taps Restriction, but Jumping Jehosephat, "The Admiral!" This was enough to break my 20 year-old heart.

I pulled what little there was left of me together, adjusted my neckerchief so nobody really read my name on my white works, and started the long march to the Admiral's cabin.

As I climbed each ladder and passed along each passageway, my heart became heavier and heavier. "My gosh," I thought, "maybe they've got something else on me!" A parade of recent sins passed through my mind. I dismissed the most heinous of these on the grounds that I had taught Sunday School for three years, and the Good Lord wouldn't let me down. Insofar as the minor sins were concerned, I couldn't for the life of me add these up to anything more than perhaps forty or fifty demerits at the outside, and even then, it would take the concerted inputs of at least five Duty Officers to pin that much on me.

By the last ladder, I was mentally writing "Statements to accompany the Conduct Reports, albeit, I was wrestling mightily with the grim fact that the clock had shown me a few minutes late for taps.

As all eternities must end, I arrived at the Admiral's Quarters. The Marine swept the curtain aside with great ceremony, and I was confronting the Flag Secretary. He looked up condescendingly as I sounded off, "Midshipman Taussig, First Class, Sir!" much as I imagined Madame LaFarge had watched the wagons rumble out of the Bastille.

"Admiral Ellis wants to see you."

Hell, I knew that. "Yes, Sir."

I was ushered before RAdm.Hayne Ellis, a very kindly gentleman with a gentle smile, and a very assured presence of understanding. He even smiled at me! "Come in, Mr. Taussig. Have a seat. I understand that you are the Midshipman-in-Charge of the Embarkation Detail."

"Yes, Sir."

"Well, I just wanted to tell you that, insofar as we can determine, this is the first ship in Practice Squadron history which is ready to weigh anchor and has every Midshipman on board that we are supposed to have, all the baggage we are supposed to have, and no supernumeraries or surpluses. I wanted to congratulate you personally."

I sat in awe for a moment. "Sir, can I make two statements?" "Certainly."

"Sir, I thought I had been called up here for breaking taps restriction last night. I was out in Smoke Park with my girl, who was leaving for California, and I violated taps. I was scared to death coming up here."

Adm. Ellis, knowing I was a Navy Junior, asked if the girl was a Navy Junior, as he might know her. So, I confessed.

"You mean Mick Carney's daughter? I don't blame you a bit. If I had a date with her I certainly would have taken the risk. And incidentally, young man, you watch Mick Carney. He's going to be Chief of Naval Operations some day. He has the most diabolical turn of mind of any young officer I have ever had the pleasure of knowing."

"Yes, sir. Sir, my second statement involves my Classmates who did the work. Actually, I have been sick all morning, and I had asked Midshipmen ...(and darned if I can remember them all today, but Jim Bartlett, Sheldon Kinney, Chuck Merdinger, and Russ Willson were four of the five I named) ...to be sure that their Divisions were taken care of. Sir, I've had diarrhea all day."

Admiral Ellis beamed. "You see, you've already learned the major lesson of leadership. All you have to do is delegate your authority."

It crossed my mind that possibly leadership could be cross-leveled, after all, with sheer inexhaustible laziness.

And so it came to pass. I left the Admiral's Quarters "golden" as the modern generation puts it. The rest of the cruise was an utter delight. We were told in La Guiara that we would graduate in February instead of June, and since I had held a "top job" already, I was seldom harassed into doing anything, until, towards the end of the cruise, I relieved Chuck Merdinger as the Midshipman Aide. This was like taking candy from a baby. Chuck was the most "organized" man I had ever known and the Office ran smoothly.

As we returned to Annapolis, it suddenly occurred to me that I was not going to be a Mustering Petty Officer. I hadn't done enough on the cruise to show how incompetently I could perform assigned duties.

Secure in this knowledge, I even started to think about "stripes." "Maybe someone can beat the aptitude system..." the thought kept recurring in my mind. I settled on two-striper. Then, an overwhelming optimism and ambition took charge of my youthful mind and kept saying "three." I saw "threes" on everything...car bumpers, first class petty officer sleeves, Ballantine Beer bottles, you name it, I saw it.

And then the roof fell in. Two days before the end of September Leave, I got a telegram to report back a day early as I was to be the Second Battalion Commander! I couldn't believe it.., and was certain my classmates wouldn't believe it.

Now, the story should always have a happy ending ... and maybe it does. On reporting, I found that the Second Battalion Officer was none other than Cdr.Jerauld Wright, fondly known to us as either "Rasputin" or "The Greet Stone Face."

At this point in time, all I will say is that I survived. Indeed, today Adm.Wright often startles me by recalling various sins I committed during First Class Year which I had, for the past 40 years, believed I'd gotten totally away with, and had been forgotten.

Some day, perhaps, I should set down the retribution that was visited on me because I had one of the loudest voices in the Class of 1941.

Joseph K.Taussig, Jr. '41

Champ or Chump (aka Sit Ups)

One day when S Company was in Halsey Field House to receive one of its numerous Plebe Summer PE tests, I witnessed the following incident. The Plebes were in pairs to see if they could do the required number of sit-ups in the allotted time. One Plebe would hold the ankles of the other and count, while the second Plebe did his sit-ups. The Plebe that counted would enter the number of his partner's sit-ups on an IBM card and then sign off on his entry.

Plebes knew the number of sit-ups that were required to pass, and they knew that if they did not pass they would have to attend a sub squad on their free time in order to build themselves up to the required number.

In one group I witnessed a young man who just missed the required number of sit-ups and was more than a bit upset. He pleaded with his partner to add a couple of sit-ups to his number so he could make the grade. He begged that he was already under too much pressure and that if he had to take free time out of his schedule to go on a sub squad, his other duties would suffer enough to get him kicked out. The partner relented at this plea for mercy, added the needed number to his score, and then signed off on the untruth.

Now, my Plebe indoctrination taught me that a naval officer was expected to have "the nicest sense of personal honor." Our Honor Concept held, "A Midshipman observing another in a dishonorable act may report the incident to the Midshipman Honor Organization directly, or he may prefer to reaffirm his observations and gain the offender's viewpoint through personal questioning prior to reporting him, or choose to caution the offender personally." So, at least I had a choice of action without incurring dishonor upon myself. Oh, ·I should mention that there was a fourth course of not dishonorable action which the Honor Concept broached, none of the above. "A Midshipman who observes an honor offense and does not take any of the above actions, has not been dishonorable and committed an honor violation himself, but has failed in his responsibility to the Honor Concept and to the Brigade."

I do not know whether it was my embarrassment at having witnessed a hitherto merciful albeit untruthful act in the guise of high crime, or my reluctance to believe that my squared-away NAPS-ter shipmate could grovel before the prospect of a sub squad, or just my newness to the whole routine, but I did nothing except think about what happened. In the due course of time, the nice Midshipman resigned from the Academy for presumably greener pastures in civilian life, while the groveler graduated with his class.

I have sometimes thought about what might have happened to this pair had I reported the obvious breech of Midshipman ethics to the culprits or the Honor Organization. Perhaps those involved would have both given me assurances that this sort of thing would never happen again, or the court of inquiry would have absolved the offenders for being yet unaccustomed to the Midshipman mold. I do not know. Yet the question has sort of nagged me through the years. Did we lose a champ and let loose a chump!

Edward DeRosa '77

Track & Field

It was the last season of intramural sports for me, the spring of my first-class year. In previous sports, I had had decent playing time in heavyweight football but was a disastrous bench-warmer in fast-pitch softball. After being cut from the plebe heavyweight crew team, I had started company basketball, at which I was a great asset to my company's team (my height was also a plus). This success slowly dwindled, however, as I moved from being a key player to being replaced by young, upstart underclassmen by my first-class year; I was lucky to get the required quarter-length playing time in some of the games.

This was hard to swallow for someone who had been a high school basketball star. This final spring there was no way I was going to sign up for any softball, even though my Dirty Thirty fast-pitch team had been a close runner-up to Eleventh Company in the championship game the previous year.

It was at this time that my second-class year roommate, Blaise Scioli, recommended that I give battalion track a try: he also happened to be the Fifth Battalion coach. They were defending champions for about the past four or five years, a budding dynasty, you might say. I was willing but had not competed in track and field since 9th grade as a miler. At this time I thought my endurance was poor and my speed moderate, but Blaise had another idea.

"We need long-jumpers." he admitted. I had done this in junior high and felt I could practice enough to be competitive. "We also badly need high-jumpers;" he added.

This I had never done. I had attempted the various jumping methods out of curiosity one afternoon when I was younger but was soon quickly discouraged. "Are you sure, Bes? I don't think I could be any good at that event," I demurred.

"You can dunk a basketball, can't you?" he challenged.

"Yes."

"Then we'll just teach you a style and have you compete. We have room for a fourth jumper, and we're going to need the points," he concluded.

So I was shuffled into the two jumping events, one at which I felt I could excel, the other just to bide my time. Nevertheless, Blaise assigned our battalion's premier intramural high-jumper, a second classman named Tom Lowry, to train me. I later learned that Tom had been instrumental in Fifth Batt's victory over Fourth for the brigade championship the year before. It seems that both teams were tied for points as the only remaining event, the high jump, was coming to a conclusion. All teammates and opponents had failed to clear the bar at 6'0" after three attempts, and Tom, on his third attempt, with officers and midshipmen from both battalions watching, made it over the bar to keep the Fifth's championship and undefeated streak intact. This was the perfect man for the job to train me; he could handle both kinds of pressure.

His technique, as was most every high-jumpers' by this time, was the Fosbury Flop, named for Dick Fosbury, who won the gold medal with it at the 1968 Olympics. It required a lot of coordination but was very smooth and easy once you mastered it, I was told.

We began with him demonstrating me his method of jumping at a moderate height. His approach was from the left but he recommended I try from the right; I experimented with both and decided eventually on a right-sided run. I felt more comfortable with a left foot takeoff than a right one. At first I went through the proper motions as he instructed me: begin from the side, turn inward, and throw your body upward off of the single foot. Once I seemed to have a handle on that, we tried the flop over the bar. These two, the jump and flight over the bar, I could not coordinate. Tom told me to imagine myself as throwing myself at the bar - the approach being the momentum I needed to lift up and then finish by thrusting my arms up at the bar, making sure my right shoulder turned into the bar to allow my body to make the back-sided Fosbury Flop over it.

This was way too much to accomplish at once. I soon began forgetting the basics Tom had given me and eventually reduced to stopping at the bar after my approach and trying to jump off both of my feet at once. Never mind that the inside knee needed to be raised while leaping upward. At this point, Tom began to make fewer and fewer comments as he stood by the pit and watched me run into the bar repeatedly. I could tell by the look on his face that he wished no one else in Halsey Field House was watching. I resigned myself to just becoming a long-jumper that would pick up some trash points for the team, by this time.

However, when the first track meet arrived, I discovered that Blaise had entered me in the high jump, regardless. Perhaps he and Tom saw something and were determined that I was going to get somewhere in this event. The meets were a single battalion vs. battalion fashion, thus allowing five track meets in the season. In the first couple of meets, I decently placed second or third consistently in the long jump. Greg "Gomez" Adams was our ace-in-the-hole in this event, usually jumping around the 22-foot mark; I don't recall him ever losing the event the whole season. My first high jump competitions, on the other hand, were fantastic fiascos; I was unable to even clear the opening height of 5'0", mostly because I could not or would not put together all of the motions. After these embarrassments, I was determined to devote all of my practice times to the high jump. Some evenings during study hour I would go into Halsey Field House and practice. I once even begged Blaise to go along with me, which he did, and critique my style.

By the third track meet I had improved. Somehow I managed to go out of the competition at 5'8"; I think I ended up placing third with this effort. Blaise and Tom were pleasantly surprised. This didn't last long, because at the fourth meet (at a time when the points were becoming more crucial late in the season), I once again failed to clear 5'0". My shoulder even hit the bar on one attempt.

"How did you do in the high jump?" Blaise asked me, then answered for me, "Tom said you screwed up. "Yeah," was my reply.

"Well, good job in the long jump," and with that, he went off to check on how the rest of the team was doing.

After that we had only one more meet to go--gut-check time and a matter of pride for me. Never mind that I had only started practicing this event a scant two months, or less, earlier. The final meet was against Fourth Batt, undefeated like us, the winner to take to Bancroft the brigade championship. It was also the same battalion Tom jumped against to narrowly edge for the championship the year before. My mind was clear and body pumped; I never expected an intramural track meet would be so important to me. In a little over a month I would be gone from this place; I needed to have just one more surge of excitement.

I had a specific take-off point I marked with white tape--three-and-a-half paces out from the right pole and twenty paces away; this distance seemed to work best for me in practice. I also took each attempt one at a time, concentrating on that height as the one and only goal. This seemed to relax me, which I was able to do even more by waiting several moments, staring at the bar, before beginning my approach. I had even developed a professional-looking quirk of raising my right heel and then rocking back on it before taking off. Proper arm swing and raising my knees while approaching were also benefits I learned with lots of practice, and I never took my eyes off of the bar!

At the final meet, I began by getting two of my three allotted long jumps out of the way. I then concentrated on the high jump and was ready when they called the competitors over. I easily cleared each height increment-5'0"-5'2"-5'4"-5'6"-5"8". I was on a roll and could feel the rush. By this time, only three jumpers remained for the 5'10" height-myself, Tom, and a small fellow from Fourth Batt who must have had springs for legs. "Fourth Batt" cleared 5'10" on the first leap, Tom on his second or third attempt; I missed my first two jumps in the meet at this height. 011e of them was with Blaise and our battalion officer standing directly behind me at my take off point. "Good jump," the colonel growled just before I left. Needless to say, it wasn't, so I blocked out all of the demons and made it on my third.

The bar moved up to 6'0"-an elusive height I was sure I, if not all three of us, would finally meet my match. I had to go first, having been the one to need more attempts to clear the last height. This allowed me no time to think and placed me at an advantage, as if I was just jumping 5'10" again. I lined up and practically pulled myself over the bar at the first attempt, my first at that height. I recall immediately jumping out of the pit and yelling at my teammate, "Come on, Tom!" I felt I had begun the spark of another spectacular win at this event again this year.

It turned out I had plenty of time to watch and wait. Tom missed his first as did "Fourth Batt"; Tom missed his second, as did "Fourth"; Tom missed his third, and "Fourth Batt" did not. Tom was eliminated, and the competition cleared the bar, lifting his feet as high as he possibly could at the end of his jump to get over that bar.

By this time, all events had completed, and quite an audience was looking on. As soon as he cleared, I immediately went over to my mar, as the field judge raised the bar to 6'2". I was unaware of the points situation or how crucial a high jump win was at the time; I did know that Dave Booth of Fourth Batt had just set an intramural shot put record and won consecutively and decisively, being the 'Greg Adams" of that event. However, now, I needed to realize that it was just me and the bar. It felt like I took little time in beginning my approach and could feel myself raise each part of my body as they passed over the bar. It was almost as if I knew its exact location as I cleared 6'2" on my first attempt.

"Holy ____!" I heard Greg Adams break the silence. I raised myself from the pit, and little Blaise met me with a tremendous bear-hug that lifted my six-foot-five-inch frame off its feet. Congratulations and a handshake from Tom Lowry I met with, "You're the one who showed me how to do it." Truer words and camaraderie were hardly equaled.

However, "Fourth Batt" still had two more tries, having missed his first. Somehow I felt I had put it out of reach, but cheers and relief did not come until he knocked the bar loose on his third try. Amid the crowding, he later found his way over to me, and shook my hand; I certainly wish I had gotten his name. I did hear he was a youngster, though, and had a couple more years to have his moment. Murmuring then began that the intramural record was 6'4", and preparations were being made for me to try to break it.

However, perhaps foolishly, I turned towards the long jump pit. I had gotten my team five points with a win at the high jump; I was going to try for more at the long jump. The adrenaline rush carried me to 20' 1", also a personal best, and second place. When I turned back to the high jump area, the field judge was gone, and everyone was heading back towards the Hall. I can only wonder what might have been. What definitely was, however, was Fifth Battalion, Intramural Track and Field Champions. On the way back, Greg mentioned to me, "Well, I guess you'll be continuing with this stuff for a while!"

Oddly enough, I never competitively jumped again, but I still have that wonderful memory. The events all still seem so clear to me, but also as if they had been only a dream. I had come out of nowhere and become the man of the hour while also keeping it a team effort.

Later that night, I went back to Halsey Field House. The bar was still set at 6'2". I went over and found my tape mark. I picked it up and sat down, staring at the bar and pondering. It all seemed unreal to me even then. Some talent, proper coaching, teamwork, and moral support had somehow made it all real.

David Hoover '84

XXII

It is ill for the winners to worry,

Take thy fate as it comes with a smile,

And when thou art safe in the harbour

They will envy, but may not revile.

Eggs is Eggs

This story, related to me by Peter Saraceni, is dedicated to his memory.

Pete and I, from different regiments at the Academy, had no contact there but met on Second Class cruise during the amphibious ship component. I was impressed by his extensive knowledge of seamanship -- particularly appropriate during amphibious operations. I never met anyone who knew as many knots as Pete did, and have had many occasions on which the truck driver' s bend, to which Pete introduced me, fit the bill as no other knot did. It is quite possible that my contact with Pete figured in my requesting deck assignments when I was ordered, after graduation, to my ships, the heavy cruisers *Macon* and *Columbus*. We did liberty together in Portugal and had a lot of experience with "scoods" (escudos, the Portuguese currency).

Anyway, we were both chow hounds and spent a lot of time fantasizing about the good foods we were not getting aboard ship. Perhaps more than other savories our conversation concerned eggs because we both loved them and hated the powdered version, the only ones "served," if that word could describe how it arrived. Having to stand (there were no seats in the enlisted mess where we ate) was bad enough. But it wouldn't have mattered that much had we had real scrambled, poached, shirred, boiled, or fried eggs.

Pete knew a junior officer in the ship's company and chatted with him from time to time. The subject of one conversation drifted to wardroom food, and eggs in particular. Asked Pete "Are you served real eggs?" "Sure." "Are they always served one way omelets or scrambled would probably be the easiest to prepare -- or can you have them any style you want?" "Any style." Pete marveled aloud and asked his friend whether he appreciated their availability. "Nah," the officer responded, "Eggs is eggs."

Pete was appalled and so was I when he told me the story. We spoke about real eggs, thought about them, dreamed of them, discussed on so many occasions variations we had experienced with descriptions of their tastes, textures, aromas, what had accompanied them, how they were served, and in delicious detail how they were savored. We hallucinated the recalled experiences in their sensed totalities. And here was this blasé plebeian with his dismissive "Eggs is eggs."

Elliott Schuman '49

Bowling for Dollars

In spite of overloading, a heavy sports schedule, and demanding military duties, some Stripers ended up with time on their hands while yearning for excitement at a time they were required to be in Bancroft Hall. Release once took the form of seeing how far a bowling ball could be bowled on the 1st Deck, starting in the corner of the 2nd Wing by the Mate's desk and trying to bowl the composition solid shot all the way to the end of the 6th Wing. Lookouts were posted to warn of OODs on the prowl and many attempts were made, most of them dying in the 4th Wing near the high-risk location of the Commandant's and Brigade Operations offices. A few would make it into the 6th Wing but peter out fairly quickly. As the 8th Wing was under construction, that attempt at distance would have to await a younger class.

A couple of Firsties were proud of their accuracy through the 4th Wing and came up with a more daring alternative. They challenged each other to see who could bowl a ball through the nightly Watch Squad formation, starting at the intersection of the same passageway above with the one running past the Brigade offices into the Rotunda, where the Watch Squad formed, and beyond into the 3rd Wing.

The protagonists studied the formation, its timing and movements, and set up dummy runs in the 2d and 4th Wings so they could get the timing exact for sending a ball through the formation at the exact moment "Open Ranks, March" had been completed and before the OOD or AOOD began the formal inspection. Again, lookouts and a clean getaway had to be organized. Obviously, many side bets were placed, with various outcomes -- ball goes awry before getting to Rotunda, ball hits Watch Squad member/rolls over "grease" shoes, ball gets through formation unscathed, ball makes it into area of Midshipman Office, ball makes it past OOD's office and further into 3d Wing, bowler caught/not caught while attempt underway, etc. The two Stripers flipped to see who would go first, with a second try to be attempted on some future, unscheduled evening.

Needless to say, in spite of trying to keep the action close to the vest, the bets grew and a substantial sum was riding when the first shot was made. No one appeared to be in the Brigade offices and the passageway lights were turned off at the Dahlgren Hall end of the 4th Wing. Lookouts gave an "all clear" and the "lucky" Firstie took up position hidden from view of the Rotunda in the 2nd-4th-6th Wing passageway by the intersection. The on-coming Midshipman Officer of the Watch (MOOW) had the squad at attention and was about to give the command "Open Ranks, March". The bowler bowled and shot out of sight. The command resounded in the passageway and the ranks opened. As the MOOW went to meet the inspecting OOD, the ball dutifully rolled down one open rank past a startled but still at attention Watch Squad, on between the MOOW and OOD, and on into the 3d Wing where it died off to the right against the Visitors Waiting Room wall across from the Midshipman Office.

By the time the OOD had reacted, all concerned had disappeared. Efforts to locate the cabal came to naught but the second attempt was dropped, as it was feared that tempting fate a second time would not end up as rosy. Don't recall who won the pool, but it wasn't me. And I can't bowl half that well!

Robert Black '63

Tooth Fairy Tales

One of the characters who sat at the Plebe football training table was Val Schaeffer, who wore number 49 and was very proud of it. He often stated that if he could score a touchdown for NAVY he would die a happy man. Need I add that he was a Navy junior.

Val wore a removable front bridge for a missing tooth, which was the result of an earlier athletic encounter with "Hambone" Hamilton, another Navy junior, when they were children. It was Val's custom to remove his tooth for meals and place it on a napkin next to his water glass until he was through. Of course, the rest of us thought this was pretty gross and let him have it in many ways.

One day the tooth disappeared and unaccountably wound up in the G.I. can reserved for scraps. It was particularly full on that day, because Val had both arms in it over his elbows. After a while amid great cheers of his classmates, he miraculously found his tooth. He then dipped it in his water glass and shoved it in his mouth. No one ever said he was fastidious. You can imagine the heat he took for that.

One of the joys of sitting on the training table was the relationship we had with the cooks, bakers and stewards. Our favorite was Purnell. He was in charge of butterfly buns, orange layer cake and cannon balls. By insuring that he always had tickets to the football games we managed to have surpluses of baked goods.

Now we're going to skip about fifty years. Val now lives on a steel-hulled wishbone ketch, much like the *Vamarie*, one of the four yachts which you, if you had a Plebe year, will remember as including the *Spindrift,*

Freedom and *Highland Light*. There was also a schooner, the *Elcubeth*. Val managed to circumnavigate the globe on his *Camalot* (don't ask why he spells it that way - but he did have a little trouble with English, in Bull class) and it only took him ten years.

It came to pass that Val needed a hip replacement, and it was accomplished in Arlington, Va., where C.M.C. Jones '49 and I thought it would be appropriate to visit. It wouldn't do to visit empty-handed so we contrived a letter from Purnell (the erstwhile chief baker) to me, which enclosed a small package.

In the letter we had Purnell recollecting that one of the guys on our training table had lost a tooth years ago and seemed to remember that he was a great football player who wore #49. In the course of a cleanup of the bakery, one of the bakers found a single tooth bridge and Purnell wondered if it might not be the tooth #49 lost and did we know how to get in touch with him.

Meanwhile, C.M.C. Jones knew a dentist who was able to provide us with a tooth for our purposes. When all preparations were complete, we went to see Val. After a lot of hand shaking, we got down to business and asked Val if he could remember who #49 was because we got the strangest letter from Purnell. Well, we were really surprised when Val told us that he was #49. So, we gave him the letter and package.

Having a brand new hip didn't silence Val at all. He went bonkers. Screamed, "That's my tooth!" Shedding a few tears, he was thrilled that Purnell could remember him after all these years. I think it was the happiest day of Val's life.

Jones and I doubled up. I couldn't tell whether Jones was laughing or crying. He was really happy to have brought such joy to the patient. I thought they were having too much fun and, after a while, spilled the beans. Val was shattered. But I thought it was fair exchange for making us look at that tooth every meal for a whole season. What goes around, comes around.

Fred Grabovsky '49

XXIII

Uncharted the rocks that surround thee,

Take heed that the channels thou learn,

Lest thy name serve to buoy for another

That shoal, the Courts Martial Return.

The USNA Experience

In your examination of Naval Academy character building, I am convinced, always have been, that character is the prime value of the USNA experience. The excellent and broad education is also of surpassing value . It would be difficult for me to identify specific experiences pleasant (many) or painful (few if any), but I'll suggest my overall impression.

The discipline, the initiation activities, are essential in preparing Naval Officers for their destiny. If a young person loses his stability and sense of humor in this process, he surely is not the person to be trusted in command of our young in storm or battle.

My own experience of the Academy was a lark -- Plebe year included. Perhaps it was because I entered young (16 1/2 years) and had no academic difficulties.

Of course the Academy experience molded my life. I entered as a citizen of a small New Jersey town, was converted to a citizen of much of the world.

In the Academy I was surrounded by contemporaries 90 % of whom I consider of well above average worth. They passed a filter which sought to assure physical, mental, and moral suitability of the input. Most of these good men have remained my friends for life -- I'm in touch with almost all my surviving classmates today.

After Navy retirement I worked as Vice President of a high-technology manufacturing company, then set up my own consulting engineering firm in Washington where I worked until 1980. This post-Navy career was built on my Navy experience and education including a degree from MIT.

In sum: I'd be pleased to have any of my family enter the USNA (with the other service academies second choice). Indeed, I'm delighted that a granddaughter just graduated from the Naval Academy.

I hope these comments are helpful

RAdm. Alfred B. Metsger '31

Memories of Plebe Year 1930-31

It was perfectly natural that I should go to the Naval Academy for the Navy was the only career I had ever contemplated, except for childhood dreams of being a fireman or an aviator. That was the only way of life I had ever known. Yet for some unknown reason, my memories of the actual entrance are rather vague. I don't recall the date in June when I first checked in, but I couldn't read 20/20 on the eye chart and was told to rest my eyes and come back in two days. On the second try there was no problem. In those days the entering Class came in by small groups through June and early July, not all on the same July day as now.

I do remember standing in line at the registration desk with a Tennessee boy between Bill Calhoun and me, a lad named B.J. Semmes. But let him tell the story, it's one of his favorites. "There I was between two guys chatting away as if I wasn't there, about people, places, and ships in the Navy. They seemed to know everything about it and I wondered how this inexperienced country boy could compete with them." There B.J. pauses, smiles slightly, and says softly, "But, you know, I was the only one of the three to graduate." He not only was graduated, he went on to vice admiral's rank.

Adm. William S. Sims, who had commanded U.S. Naval Forces, Europe during World War I and was one of the Navy's most distinguished officers, happened to be visiting in Annapolis the day my group was sworn in as Midshipmen, in Memorial Hall beneath Perry's "Don't give up the ship" flag. The Admiral gave us a very inspirational talk, of which the only bit I remember was that the Navy had taught him patience, a characteristic much to be desired. How? He had spent 40 years in the Navy, and 30 of them waiting for boats. Another memory is being checked for swimming qualifications by coach Henry Ortland. I was fine at crawl, back and sidestrokes but a failure at breast stroke because I was using a scissors kick. Coach Ortland yelled at me, "Who taught you how to swim?" I answered, "You did, sir, in the Navy junior class in 1921." Henry grinned, told me to try again with a proper kick, and passed me through.

With the wisdom of youth I thought that I'd had enough Spanish from my time in the Philippines (all I really knew was the pronunciation) so I'd better master another language at the Academy and chose French. That put me in the Fourth Battalion with Jack Woodruff, also from Severn, as my Plebe Summer roommate. It wasn't long before he was picked up for some minor offense and went to the *Reina Mercedes* for a week. She was one of the Spanish cruisers sunk at Santiago, raised after the war and brought to the States, and fitted out to be the Receiving Ship for the Naval Academy, where she also served as confinement barracks for deserving Midshipmen. By the end of the first day I got very lonely in that double room, for we had not had time to make new friends and visiting was strictly limited. Although I didn't smoke then, I lit a borrowed cigarette, walked into the Rotunda, and immediately joined Jack in the ship.

The *Reina Mercedes* was to become a familiar home, for I was destined to spend a lot of time in her Midshipmen quarters, along with some very good friends. We marched to and from Bancroft Hall to join our unrestricted Classmates for classes and drills but spent all the rest of our time on board. We had our own mess, served from the crew's general mess, a couple of living and studying compartments below decks, and we all slept in hammocks slung six feet above the main deck. These were not the garden variety of hammock, but Navy issue, heavy canvas just over six feet long and about four wide. They were attached to hammock hooks set in the overhead beams and pulled up tight, so that they curled up and resembled oversized cylinders hung in the air in horizontal rows. To climb in, one grabbed the overhead beam and swung his legs up and over, sliding down into the nest -- and a very comfortable nest it was once inside. Of course, there were the few who tried to sit up or perform some other foolishness and ended up sadder but wiser on the deck below. There were a couple of hospital visits for concussion or broken bones, but most of us learned quickly and enjoyed excellent sleeping.

There were two heads on the berthing deck. One was labeled "Enlisted" for the crew, the other was for "Midshipman Olny (sic)." We never did find out who he was but were glad to make use of his facility.

Just at that time a great scandal erupted among the Second Classmen, who spent the Summer at the Academy for various purposes. One had managed to keep a local girl in his Bancroft Hall room overnight and, too enthused by that success, dressed her in White Works and took her down to breakfast in the Mess Hall. Unfortunately for him, a duty officer passed by, noticed the long hair and blew the whistle. The Midshipman was dismissed (he was later graduated from college and commissioned in the Marine Corps a few days ahead of the Academy Classmates), but the Classmate who was in charge of good order at the table was reported for negligence of duty in not reporting the violation and promptly joined us in the *Reina*. That was where RAdm. Francis Foley and I first became good friends.

Two of my Classmates created an attention-grabber when they put up their nameplates over the door to their room in Bancroft. One was Sapp, the other Nutt. Now Johnny Sapp was a good level-headed lad who eventually made Marine Colonel but some of us thought Stan Nutt earned his name. When working the target butts on the rifle range, instead of pulling them down by the bolt rope hung below each target, safely below the line of fire, he would grab the bottom of the target itself and yank it down. By sheer luck he never got a rifle bullet through his hand, but his system was not very bright. After graduation he dropped the "Nutt" and settled on his first two names of "Stanley Tyler," but he may also have dropped his luck for he was killed not long afterwards in a plane crash.

Another Classmate, Willie Buess, and I became great pals that summer and went on to be Academic Year roommates. What a guy! He was short and squatty with tremendous upper body strength and had never seen a lacrosse stick before coming to Annapolis, but made goalie on the Plebe team come Spring. He could do 100 push-ups with no difficulty; whenever told to do 34 (the standard punishment for minor upsets to Upper Classmen was push-ups to your Class number) he would comply and then ask politely, "shall I do another 34, sir?" It was a great loss when Willie failed his math re-exam after Summer Cruise and departed for Trinity College, where he was graduated and made the Dean's list in math -- or so I was told.

The Class of 1932 was enjoying (?) Aviation Summer at the Academy while '31 and '33 were off on a European cruise. The aviation part, as we lived it two years later, consisted of five or six observation flights in the nose of an experimental seaplane that later became the famed *Catalina* of World War II, and five days disassembling, assembling, and shooting aircraft machine guns on the rifle range. Some, those with good conduct records, were detailed as instructors for the new Plebes, the rest did engineering laboratory work. One bonus was every other weekend out-of-town liberty, then a prized treasure never before experienced. After the weekday evening meal most Mids of both Classes congregated in Smoke Park, just outside the Mess Hall, for rest and relaxation, especially one Jack Counihan '32. He stopped Willie and me one evening for a little verbal running; a torrent of professional questions when "I don't know" was not an acceptable response, no matter how true. We had to think of some answer, the wilder the better. Willie and I enjoyed that interchange enough so that most nights from then on we'd parade by his park bench just to be run by him -- and vice versa as far as we were concerned. That began a lifelong friendship with Captain Jack.

Throughout Plebe Summer we were told of what horrors to expect when the Upper Classes came back to start the new year, and we also heard stories of the dreadful tricks played on innocent Midshipmen by duty officers. One "Red" Magruder (Later Commodore Cary Magruder USN '08) first became famous for reporting those standing in the barbershop line for "Hair, not properly cut." Then, in making rounds around Bancroft Hall during study hours, he would order the Mate-of-the-Deck to pass the word, "Son-of-a-bitch Red Magruder is aboard." Naturally people stuck their heads out of their doors to see what was going on, and Red reported them all for leaving their rooms during study hour without permission. One day an experienced Mate saw him coming and passed the fatal word without having been told to do so. Red put him on the report for insubordination – "Who gave you permission to call me 'Red'?"

Another D.O. one Sunday evening came to a Midshipman room with no light showing. He knocked on the door and pushed in as two sleepy Mids were tumbling out of their bunks. He gave them a hard time for not studying and a 20-minute lecture on the vital importance of class standing to career opportunities, promotion and pay. Finally he finished and asked the nearer of the two, "And where did you stand in your Class last year?' "First, sir." The then speechless D.O. turned and fled.

For the Academic Year Willie and I ended up in the Eighth Company of the Fourth Battalion; there were then only eight with a maximum enrollment of about 1,800 Midshipmen, and four battalion wings comprised Bancroft Hall. Since the Eighth Company was always the last to march on or off the field for any parade, and company formations were arranged in order of individual heights, the shortest man in the Eighth Company was always the last man on and off field. For three of our four years dubious honor was held by "Brute" Krulak, who overcame that apparent handicap by being elected captain of the crew as a First Classman and making lieutenant general in the Marine Corps.

The Upper Class did come back and each First Classman selected a Plebe or two as "his," meaning that he was responsible for training, discipline and sometimes protection of the Plebe while the Plebe was available for friendly running and occasional errands -- such as tearing up another First Classman's room in his absence. Then the hazing began, which was only done by First Classmen until white cap covers came back to uniform in the Spring, when Youngsters were given a hand in the game. Until then the Youngsters were not much more than Plebes "carrying on" (ignoring Plebe "rates" such as walking down the center of corridors and turning square corners, and sitting on the front two inches of the mess hall chair with four buttons of the six showing above the table). One of the hazing tricks was the "swim to Baltimore." Between each room and its clothes closet was a small open window space with a sill about six inches wide. The Plebe had to balance his belt on that sill, stretch out at full length, and swim the crawl stroke. One stroke was a yard and Baltimore was a thousand yards away, so nobody ever got there, but it was good exercise.

Another game was "Battle Practice," where one Plebe with trousers at half mast bent over horizontally as the gun, another stood by his head with a handful of talcum powder, a third stood left and rear as first loader, and the fourth stood right and rear as gun captain with a wet sponge in hand. A First Classman stood by with a broom. On the commands, "Ready, Aim, Fire" he would whack the gun's rear with the broom, the gun made a loud "boom" sound, the powderman blew off the talcum to make smoke, the gun captain would ram the wet sponge against the gun's breech and yell "Bore clear." and the loader would ram his fist against the wet spot and report, "Ready Two." Whereupon all the Plebes would rotate stations for the next round. With a good-humored Firstie, the game could be and often was fun as it was meant to be, for the broom never really hurt. It never dawned on us that it might be degrading; all we were thinking about was when we would become First Classmen.

The beginning of Academic Year brought something new. At Severn we had learned to study, to dig out the material on our own, but we had never been exposed to the instructor's one-breath "Are there any questions? Draw slips and man the boards." We marched to and from every class in our recitation sections, took seats in the classroom and, on command (since there was never time for any question) drew our slips. On the instructor's desk, upside down, was a typed question for each student; which he took to the blackboard and proceeded to write out his answer. Each day's work was graded, and the "dailies" counted 60 percent against the monthly exams, 40 percent of the monthly grade. Typical "slips" I remember from later years were "Describe the terms of the Treaty of Ghent," and "Sketch and describe a Curtis high pressure turbine." If we were lucky the instructor would answer questions if time remained after the recitations, but that was not always helpful because most of the young naval officer instructors had no teaching experience nor were they often experts in their subjects. Most were just trying to stay one lesson ahead of their students.

In just about every Naval Academy class there are at least one or two scions of West Point graduates and it was traditional that they would be selected for the beneficial job of scrubbing the Navy Goat every Friday night before football games. The two goat keepers in '31 were "Long John" and "Uncle Charlie" Kirkpatrick (no relations); they did the selecting and supervised the scrub job in the goat's weekend quarters in the enclosed courtyard of the Third Battalion wing of Bancroft Hall. "Long John" lived across the hall from me. Whether he was too lazy to look or there was no Army brat in '34, I don't know but he picked me as a Navy junior and thus next best to be the scrubber. Every Friday afternoon I'd make my way down to the courtyard and wrestle with Bill, who did not like baths, to get him clean for the morrow's game. My own shower afterwards never quite removed the aroma of goat, which I got used to but classmates and neighbors did not. But the job was beneficial; Bill looked bright and clean for the game and I rated carrying on through dinner that evening. Even one night off from being a Plebe at table was very welcome.

There were then two swimming pools in the Academy, a small one in MacDonough Hall loaded with chlorine, known as the "cesspool," used for basic instruction and recreation, and the intercollegiate 50-yard pool in the Natatorium used by the swimming and water polo teams, and for advanced instruction. No Plebe could use the big pool unless he was on one of the two team squads. I hated the cesspool but couldn't swim fast enough for the swimming team, so I went out for water polo. In those days it was played with a soft ball that could be taken under water so most of the game was played down below, out of sight of the referee. We were known as the "Suicide Squad" but it was good fun, resulted in many solid friendships, and got me onto the training table for the Winter semester of Plebe Year, away from Plebe rates and running and with much better menus than in the regular mess.

When the season ended, coming back to the regular table as a Plebe was a rude shock, especially because it was headed by one Deatley Ingalls Davis, a First Classman who had a strong dislike for me -- he thought, with some justice, that I was "ratey." That was proven at dinner one evening when he asked me a professional question in navigation: "Mr. Smith, what is the vulgar establishment of the Naval Academy?" Never having had any occasion to deal with a vulgar establishment in all of my later navigation duties, I'm not sure what it is other than having something to do with the time interval between the moon's meridian crossing and the next full moon. At that time I hadn't the foggiest idea of what it was but, not allowed an "I don't know," I answered,

"Sir, it's the Batt Office." For that I was ordered to finish my meal under the table, between other diners' feet, which was not too bad because there was no running down there. What was bad was that I thought it would be a good idea to put a butter coating on Mr. Davis' shoes, and proceeded to do so.

Then came the Masqueraders show, one of the few occasions when a Plebe could have a date. Davis asked me if I was dragging and, when I said yes, ordered me to go to the barber shop and have my head clean shaved. That seemed a bit much so I appealed to my First Classman, Gus Wilson. He took me to Rex Hain, the company commander, who also though it a bit too much. Rex told me to forget the order, and he told off Davis, which did me a lot of no good with him.

Deatley Davis was an unfortunate soul. His brother was the First Captain and a top man academically at West Point, very popular with all hands, and his sister was a lovely, friendly and attractive girl who was also very popular. Deatley, on the other hand, stood 11 from the bottom of his Class, had no regimental rank, and was not very popular even among his own classmates. Apparently he felt that comparison very deeply and suffered from a Napoleonic complex trying to overcome it. Too bad.

At Easter time the Regiment shifted from blue back to white cap covers and the Youngsters acquired hazing rights. They brought us something new, the midnight shower. A gaggle of '33s would come into the Plebe room, wake up the occupants, and shove them, pajamas and all, into the cold shower. Next came a firm paddling with a wooden clog shoe to warm up the shivering sufferer, who was then carefully tucked into bed with the covers worked tightly around him so that the whole bed was soaked also. This went on two or three times a week until the Youngsters tired of the sport. Why nobody caught pneumonia I'll never know, except that we were all very healthy young men.

In our case the gaggle of '33s consisted of lads who have been close friends ever since. About half of them "spooned" on Willie, the other half on me. An Upper Classman spooned on a Plebe by shaking hands with him, after which they were equals with no rates between them. On entering our room the group divided, those who spooned on me taking care of Willie and vice versa. One night I was being aroused and sleepily held up a hand for a pull up out of bed. The Youngster took my hand and pulled, and I suddenly realized that his handclasp constituted a spoon, even though inadvertent. He refused to recognize it and I refused not to, which made no difference at the moment because his classmates took care of the festivities. But the question of whether or not it was a legitimate spoon divided the Fourth Battalion Youngsters into two camps until the approach of June Week made it a moot point.

Late that Spring, mother came to Annapolis to visit grandmother and brought younger sister Lou along, Mother and Lou were both after me to get her a Midshipman date, which I refused to do on grounds that she was too young at 14 and that my classmates couldn't have dates anyhow. So she walked down to lacrosse practice, an extravagantly pretty young blonde, and came home glowing with excitement. She had met a Midshipman, not any Midshipman but a First Classman with three stripes, and he had invited her to the hop that Saturday. He also turned out to be my company commander, a fact that neither mother nor Lou have ever let me forget. Lou went to the hop but, having to act considerably older than her age, was so nervous that she didn't really enjoy the evening.

That Saturday I came out to grandmother's for lunch, after which mother told me that an old school friend of hers was in town with her daughter. I was invited to go along with mother to meet the daughter and perhaps show her around. At that I hastily excused myself as being in charge of room and having to get right back to Bancroft Hall. In the Fall, as a Youngster, without a date, I dropped in at a hop to look over the field for cut-in dances. That was the way hops were run, everybody danced with people other than the escorted date to the enjoyment of both sides. Too bad that custom disappeared in favor of the one-and-only approach. On the floor was a friendly First Classman, Yank Meader, dancing with the most beautiful girl I'd ever seen. I dashed below and tapped Yank's shoulder for a cut-in. He started to introduce me but she stopped him as soon as he had mentioned my name and proceeded to tell me my life's history. I was flabbergasted. It turned out that she was the school friend's daughter I had turned down six months before, and it was six more months before she could arrange to have a weekend date with me. Her name was Clayton Estes, then a solo dancer in Broadway shows, but she married a lad in '32 and I never saw her again.

Finally came June Week, "No mo' rivers," and the end of Plebe Year. Also came the word that RAdm. Thomas Hart would relieve RAdm. Samuel Robison as Superintendent on 31 May. Rumor had it that Admiral Robison had been too easygoing and Hart was being sent in to take up the slack. Apparently so did some of the First Class because at daylight on 31 May all the Plebes were ordered outside to festoon the trees in Smoke Park with streamers of toilet paper. That was fun and it was quite an impressive sight when we were done, but not one that was appreciated by the authorities. It was not the First

Classmen who had given the order, but the Plebes who carried it out who spent the rest of the day clearing up all the mess.

June Week was a jumble of changing uniforms, parades, a few Army-Navy marches, a lot of girls dragged by a lot of Midshipmen but not by me and, finally, graduation. The speakers usually predict that what they say on that day will not be remembered; that is quite true but neither are most of the speakers. My only real memories are marching home from the last parade with reversed and sloped arms, and standing around the seawall with seabags at the ready the day after graduation, waiting for boats to take us out to the battleships *Arkansas* and *Wyoming* for our three-month Summer cruise. And what a cruise! Copenhagen with a side trip to Berlin, Glasgow with trips around Scotland, Cadiz with a side trip to Madrid, Gibraltar with a side trip to Tangier, and home to Norfolk before the gunnery shoot on the Southern Drill Grounds.

Roy C. Smith, III '34

Electrical Science & Mother Bancroft

Many a Mid has put hard-earned knowledge about "juice" to use in ways not really intended and, although technology has changed, the results in this episode could have happened in any era in Bancroft Hall.

A pair of Firsties, allegedly from the Class of 1935, roomed together on an upper deck of the 3rd Wing diagonally across from the elevator, which Midshipmen were prohibited from using for their personal ups and downs. Officers could and did use it regularly.

This pair decided to put their own controls on the system and proceeded to secrete wires from the control panel in the basement of the Third Wing to the desk in their room.

Desks in those days were simple tables of wood with sliding drawers. The Firsties hollowed out one of the legs on a lathe over at Isherwood, ran the wires up the leg to a switch hidden under the desktop, and then could turn the power to the elevator on and off at will.

They soon put their new convenience to use when a Company Officer went to use the elevator enroute to a meeting elsewhere in Bancroft Hall. As soon as the elevator left the deck, the Firsties switched the power off, halting it between decks. Anguished cries from the trapped officer could be heard and alert Mates of the Deck sent multiple calls through the Watch resulting in Public Works responding to the trouble.

As the electricians arrived on scene, our erstwhile Firsties turned the power back on and the elevator continued to a proper halt at the next deck, whereon the irate officer alighted and stormed off.

The electricians were unable to find anything wrong and returned to Public Works, as the Firsties' job on the equipment remained undetected. They kept up their fun and games for awhile until they decided discretion was the better part of valor and disconnected their rig before being discovered.

Robert A. Black '35

Who Killed the Navy Goat?

In the fall of 1945, ten days before the Army-Navy game, Billy the Goat was found dead in the courtyard of Bancroft hall. There was no backup goat readily available at the time. Having heard about the tragedy, the Governor of Texas saved the day by sending the Academy a fine Texas goat to serve as a replacement mascot. The goat, accompanied by no less than Miss Texas 1945, arrived by plane in time for the Army Game.

Until now the death of Billy the Goat remained a mystery. Mel Davis, Bob Gilliland and Ham Perkins, all boys from the South, lived together in Bancroft Hall. Mel's mom sent a Southern style coconut cake to these three starving Plebes. After a long, hot train ride, the cake had turned rancid and was inedible. So Mell threw the cake out the window into the courtyard. Billy the Goat immediately devoured this Southern delicacy and dropped dead on the spot – where he was found the next day.

Ham Perkins '49

XXIV

Though Armour, the belt that protects her.

The ship bears the scar on her side;

It is well if the court acquit thee;

It were best hadst thou never been tried.

Collision At Sea

One of my fellow Plebe sailing instructors during the summer of '88 was a classmate by the name of Rich Hernandez. During one of our classes, bobbing around on the Severn River, Rich's crew just happened to consist of all female 4th class-persons, affectionately known as "Plebettes." This was an unusual occurrence because the boat assignments were always made randomly.

During the at-sea exercise, Rich's mind – certainly his eyes – must have wandered because suddenly and without warning, while executing a jibing maneuver, there was another knockabout dead ahead. With no time to react, Rich's craft was hit broadside, throwing all crew members overboard.

No one was injured and no one was lost at sea. The Plebettes' swimming skills were duly tested and all hands were rescued by nearby knockabouts. The disabled craft was towed back to Santee Basin and Rich and his scattered crew were justifiably embarrassed, but a bit more alert than ever before.

The following day, as the instructors assembled to prepare for the next sailing lesson, I noticed the empty boat slip in Santee Basin. It was readily apparent that the damage to the knockabout was more serious than we had thought, and the small craft was permanently retired from duty. I understood how spectators must feel as the *Blue Angels* do a fly-by with one open spot in their formation in memory of a fallen brethren.

Thinking back, I don't recall any other excursions that summer in which all crew members in a single knockabout were Plebettes.

Tom Williams '88

Same Story, Different Perspective

As I remember it from the captain's chair on the bridge of Knockabout 7... the weather was perfect, the seas calm, a slight westerly breeze, the water warm and the sun setting at our backs. We had just finished teaching the basics of sailing, when it was time to step in to the world of naval combat. Immediately oars became cannons. The crew of Knockabout 7 easily mastered the siphoning effect of drawing water into the oar and discharging it on command. Now we needed a target. After a couple of passive returns from some of the other boats, we spied the worthy knockabout X. It's admiral and captain were duly noted for their fierce fighting techniques and hand to hand combat. Our goal was to continuously cross the T. Firing broadsides into their stern, we engaged. Both plebe crews fought valiantly. We even captured an oar along the way. As we maneuvered around a spectating knockabout, knockabout X reengaged. The fight was upon us. Knockabout X closed skillfully to cross the T. We turned and passed port to starboard thus bringing the full wrath of a days worth of training down on upon each other.

Feeling that we had handily won the battle we veered off, leaving our victims on the leeward side. As tacked off into the setting sun, victory in hand, all hands reading the tattletales on the sails. We were viciously rammed. The bow of knockabout X crossed our beam, instantly knocking our winch into the deep recesses of the dark and unknown bilge. The crew pulled together and Knockabout 7 limped into port. Although Knockabout 7 won the battle, we had lost the war.

Forever, no one will remember the skill, the bravery and the cunning of the 7 crew. In fact, all they remember is that Rich's knockabout wasn't in his slip the next day. No one asked, how did the winch get knocked in? No one cares of the storms that were encountered. They only care if you brought the ship into port. It was a valuable lesson I learned that day: it is not whether you win or lose, but can you sail the next day that counts.

Rich Hernandez '88

The Sea Anchor

One of the enjoyable exercises for Plebes was learning small craft seamanship sailing the sloop-rigged knockabouts. These were abbreviated sailboats measuring roughly 16 feet at the waterline. The Academy maintained about 30 of these, tied up in Santee Basin and, as I recall, five Midshipmen were assigned to each boat in order to be trained in hoisting and trimming the sails, handling the lines and tiller, tacking, coming about, jibing and other things nautical. On the weekends, upper classmen could check out a knockabout to enjoy a few hours of sailing with their drags (dates).

During Plebe summer, knockabout training was part of the curriculum and there was a staff of experienced instructors available to conduct this training. In 1954 I was a young Lieutenant assigned as an instructor in the Seamanship and Navigation Department, and among my many duties was to oversee the knockabout program. Once the Plebes had mastered the basics, we would hone their skills by holding knockabout races on the Severn River. And in those days Knockabout # 13 had a reputation as being the fastest of the fleet. It looked like all the others, was rigged similarly, but for some reason unknown to any of us on the Seamanship and Navigation staff, # 13 just moved considerably faster through the water than any of its sister craft.

One of the other S&N staff members was an enlisted Petty Officer by the name of Doggie Winters. Doggie was a salty character, very experienced, confident in his abilities and extremely competitive by nature. During one of these seamanship classes when another of our knockabout races was planned, the crew assignments called for Doggie to command # 13. In his inimitable style, Doggie predicted victory by five boat lengths and was giving odds on anyone foolish enough to bet against him. However, we had a mischievous plan to fix the race. While I distracted Doggie's attention, another staff member tossed a galvanized bucket into the water and secured its tether to one of the shrouds near the stern of # 13.

As we cast off and started to make way out of Santee Basin heading for the first marker buoy, Doggie was frustrated that his knockabout wasn't responding properly. All the other boats were already out of the basin when # 13 had barely left the slip. It wasn't long before Doggie suspected foul play, found the sea anchor and corrected the problem. But by then his one-knot speed advantage was not enough to overtake the lead boat.

Of course, no one confessed to the misdeed. Doggie didn't want to draw attention to the handicap that, had he been more observant, should have been noticed before the race began. The clear favorite lost its long-standing record and Doggie, who was sharp enough to make it a close race in any other craft, had all he could do not to come in last.

You can bet your sheepshank that Doggie never again let his guard down. This was a lesson for Doggie, and for the rest of us as well. Beware: sometimes in life an overlooked detail can completely upset the expected course of events!

Tom Seelye '49

Knocking About in Knock-Abouts

The second episode didn't hold such dire consequences, but still was a blow to our pride and we learned never to take the sea too lightly. Now it was in the spring of our Plebe year and once again the urge for feminine companionship was racing through our veins. Two of my good friends from high school, Kit Reinier and Bob Packenham, were studying at American University in D. C. I called them and arranged for them to bring to coeds posing as their dates, but in reality potential companions for us next year. To show off our newly learned sailing skills, we decided to take them all four of them out on the Chesapeake. Surely a day of skimming across the beautiful bay would be impressive to the ladies in particular.

Wrong!!! As we were coming in, a sharp stiff squall kicked up churning up the waves and making the approach to the cove where the boats were docked a difficult one. I had the conn and Dick was handling the sails. I told him I would turn into the wind and as I did he would drop the mainsail.

Hopefully our momentum would take us into the dock for a sweet landing. I made a port turn into the sailing cove, just as a burst of wind came from another direction. This put us on a starboard tack instead of heading into the wind, thereby increasing rather than decreasing our speed. I was yelling at Dick to get the mainsail down, but with the wind so strong, he couldn't get the cleat undone. Suddenly I realized we were going to hit the dock at ramming speed. I decided to make one more valiant effort to stem this disaster. I hooked my legs onto the stern of the boat and grabbed the bollard as we went whizzing by at full speed. Had I been as schooled in mass and momentum as I should have been, I would have realized this attempt was futile. Suddenly there I was, slowly sliding down the bollard into the water, watching our knockabout hit the dock with a resounding crash along with the sounds of a splintering bow. My friends, not realizing the critical situation, were in stitches at the bumbling of their two Academy friends. The girls were totally unimpressed; we were mortified at best.

Once again the Gods were with us as the Dockmaster had seen the change in direction of the wind and our valiant attempt at stopping damage to the boat, so he let us off with an adage that sticks with me today: 'Never take the sea for granted. She is a fickle mistress. I think we both learned a lesson that day that has served us both well.

As an interesting follow on to the latter story, eight years later I was stationed in Panama. My friend Bob Packenham had just completed a two-year study in Brazil in preparation for his Ph.D. thesis. I invited him to go water skiing on Gatun Lake. To make a long story short, we ran aground bending the propeller and had to row our boat for four hours in a heavy downpour to pull the boat out of the water. It, therefore, will be of little surprise to note than when I became qualified in submarines and offered to take then Dr. Packenham, a professor sub for a day, he quickly and emphatically declined.

Dick became a four star Admiral, having served as CO of the Eisenhower, CVN - 69, and rising to the position of CINCPACFLT. I became a Captain and had my CO tour as a commander of a Defense Contracting Agency. More times, I'm sure, we both looked back on these two experiences during Plebe year, and were glad they happened then and not later in our careers As one of our most famous nautical quotations goes, "A collision at sea can ruin your entire day." That goes for ramming docks as well.

Bob Osmon '60

XXV

Take heed in your manner of speaking,

That the language ye use may be sound;

In the list of the words of your choosing,

"Impossible" may not be found.

Speaking Before Thinking

Early in Plebe year, while serving as messenger on watch, I was sent to another Battalion Office by Midshipman Office of the Watch (MOOW) St. George '47, a fearsome four-striper.

I entered the Battalion Office, stood at attention and "sounded off" properly, but was very nervous. When asked my business, I responded, "Saint Peter sent me." And brought down the house with laughter.

Tom Watkins, '49

Beat Navy, Sir!

As a brand-new Plebe, learning to get around Bancroft Hall was often a difficult and exhausting experience. Difficult because it is perhaps the largest dormitory in the world and exhausting because everywhere you went, through all 4.8 miles of corridors and 33 acres of floor space, you had to chop.

Chopping is a bit like running up a ladder without the benefit of the ladder. You wind up moving horizontally in an exaggerated, vertical hop. With each step your knees are supposed to come as high as your chest and your elbows stay tucked against your ribs, arms bent and forearms out in front of you, leading the way. You move about in this manner with your chin tucked back into your neck and you look like an animated pogo stick.

To add to the effect, you square all of your corners at right angles and sound off alternating the phrases "Go Navy, Sir!" and "Beat Army, Sir!" with each course change. This sounds simple, and you can bet you look pretty simple doing it, but for the newly minted Fourth Class Midshipman it is an easy thing to lose your breath and jumble your words. I did it several times that first week, saying everything from "Navy, Navy, Sir!" and "Go Sir!" to "Sir, Sir!"

Each time I carelessly shouted one of these disjointed phrases while catching my breath I knew that one day I was going to get caught. One slip of the tongue was going to cost me an afternoon outside some upperclassman's doorway. Sure enough, early one afternoon it happened after noon meal. As I reached the top of the stairs to the third deck five flights in all from the mess hall I squared the corner to go into the passageway leading to my room, and

252

in a frantic rush of breath I yelped "Go Army, Sir!" The second it left my throat I knew I was done for. A First Class Midshipman stopped me dead in my tracks, fuming that some brand-new Plebe would voluntarily say such a blasphemous thing.

At that point in a Plebe's life all he knows, all he is allowed to know, is that he must chop, memorize and regurgitate facts, and Beat Army. Before he could say another word I threw out my hand and loudly requested permission to retract my last statement. Not only did he give me the opportunity to do so; he thought it best that I take the whole thing back. So for the remainder of the day I chopped backwards down the passageways of Bancroft Hall, shouting "Sir, Navy Go!" and "Sir, Army Beat!"

Jeff Conklin '93

Loose Lips Sink Ships *(and relation-ships)*

Navy wives seem to come with a built-in sixth-sense – a kind of radar about stories, gossip or tidbits that fill in the missing pieces of times their spouses or lovers are at sea or otherwise out of sight.

Such prescience was demonstrated during my ten-year reunion, specifically at the Tailgate party. For those who've been there, done that, it will come as no surprise that the tales of wild days in Bancroft Hall flow more easily with each brew that's consumed, and few of those recounting these exploits bother to be on guard or to even be aware who may be listening in. Well it was during this Tailgater that the wife of a classmate noticed her husband engrossed in a stimulating conversation with another former (female) Midshipman. The bits of conversation she overheard made it clear that our friend had had more than a professional relationship with the woman. It seems that her hubby, while he was a Midshipman – and more importantly while the two of them were "an item" – allegedly slept with the distaff middy, but she never knew it and neither did his roommate. She figured it out and, needless to say, became very upset in the midst of this weekend of high camaraderie, bravado and good times.

On the ride back to the hotel she accused him of the indiscretion. Of course he denied it vehemently, saying she was crazy for thinking that of him. Even his former roommate, who was also in the car with them, defended his buddy. But his wife didn't let up. She ranted, she raved, she screamed and pitched a fit. He figured it couldn't get any worse even if he confessed to the long-forgotten affair, so that's exactly what he did. But he was wrong....it **did** get worse!.

Naturally the wife was pissed, the buddy was shocked, the weekend was a washout, and my classmate cursed the day he ever decided to attend the big reunion. Their names have been withheld to protect the not-so-innocent.

Tom Williams '88

The President of Alabama

After three years of confinement, the Mids were granted an overnight by the Academy Superintendent, Admiral Holloway. On a beautiful fall morning in 1948, Ham perkins and Jim McVoy were standing in uniform like two "eager beavers" at 6 a.m. on Sunday in front of the old Washington Hotel (rooms then were $6.00 per night), when they were startled to see the "Commander in Chief" striding directly toward them from the Treasury Building across the street.

He was accompanied by several "Dick Tracy" types in trench coats (with weapons hidden underneath, no doubt). The two Mids snapped to attention and braced up like Plebes (shoulders back, chin in, gut in, fanny tucked) while rendering a snappy salute.

In response to their "Good Morning, Mr. President," President Truman cheerfully asked, "Where are you boys from?" They replied "Birmingham, Alabama, Sir."

The President looked at them and said, "They don't like the President very much down in Alabama. Do they?"

They saluted again and Ham said, "Mr. President, Sir, you are the President of Alabama too, Sir."

The President and his Secret Service agents all laughed heartily as they proceeded down Pennsylvania Avenue.

Note (1) In 1948, there was a Dixiecrat revolt in Congress challenging the President.

Note (2) President Truman's Missouri grandparents are reported to have fondly remembered the Confederate Army.

Ham Perkins '49

XXVI

As the wave rises clear to the hawse pipe,

Washes aft, and is lost in the wake.

So shall ye drop astern, all unheeded,

Such time as the law ye forsake.

Cool Cats

In an epic moment during World War II, Rear Admiral Mare Mitscher gave the famous command to "turn on the lights" to aid his victorious but tired pilots find their way back to their carriers. The Japanese Navy was still a threat, nightfall was upon them and the Admiral knew his pilots were maneuvering aircraft that were literally flying on fumes. It was a bold move equal to those of Nelson or Farragut and an excellent lesson in command to be learned by all future Naval Officers. This is a story about turning on a different type of electrical device that required the audacity of Mitscher and all the instinct of survival.

It all began around a month before our Firsties were about to leave us behind. My roommates, Steve "Sam" Savery from Florida and John "Ruptser" Rupp from Long Island and myself were all looking forward to the imminent arrival of the long prayed-for climbing of Herndon monument and regaining some of our inalienable rights that were so quickly forfeited the previous July.

The sun was quickly setting on our Plebe year as signs of a return to civility were already evident. The earlier trials and tribulations endured by my classmates were fast becoming "fond" memories. The daily rates had long since been any sort of challenge. One quick glance at the weekly menu sheet and the entire entree for the day was memorized. The all important "Days" we had to keep tally of were all within 30 days and no longer required much thought to recite. All OOD's and their billets were easily retractable from our cerebrumic storage file.

Besides, as "May madness" descended on Canoe U, our daily rates, for so long our core of survival in the Brigade, seemed less important as final exams approached and the Brigade, itself, had more important things on its mind than harassing the servient Plebes. Firsties had graduation and weddings on their minds and were counting their own "days" to the start of flight school, SWAS, nuke training, and The Basic School. The fearless Segundos had their Ring Dance and First Class cruise awaiting them; while the Youngsters were content to peacefully ride out their "year off" and just be observers of the Commissioning Week's activities. Even come arounds were much kinder and gentler. By now, they were more or less a formality than a character building exercise, usually just being asked the main course of the menu before being told to "shove off."

Even the approaching final exams appeared to be of little threat to my happy Plebe room as all three of us were looking sound academically. Steve (who was baptized the name 'Sam' during an intramural football game when someone told our team captain that his name was Sam), was a pure genius who would study about an hour each night so as to not make me and John feel bad. John and I were both challenged by the academics but felt optimistic that a good performance on exams would net us both a 3.0 average.

Yes, life was good for me and my fellow two musketeers during our final days of Plebedom; nothing but blue skies and fair winds to Youngsterville. Then it happened. A virtual powder keg of explosives was delivered to our room. The day started out simple enough; the three of us were in our room studying when suddenly a couple of janitors came in and installed an air conditioner! After the janitors left, the three of us just stood there scratching our heads, silently staring at our new piece of government-issue.

It was a scene reminiscent of the apes staring at the monolith in "2001: A Space Odyssey." What came next was the interesting debate of "Do we turn it on?" "Do we rate an air conditioner in our room?" "If we use it, will we have to pay the electrical bill?" "What does the MHP say?" Suddenly, classmates and upper classmen alike were peeking in our once inconspicuous room to see our new piece of furniture.

What was supposed to be a smooth final approach to Herndon had hit severe cross winds as this seemingly authorized but very un-Plebe-like temptation stood before us. After a short discussion, we despondently agreed not to use the air conditioner as we initially guessed that they probably installed it in the wrong room; and to turn it on would incur the wrath of our chain-of-command all the way from Youngster to the Secretary of Navy. Besides, Herndon was less than a month away and neither of us saw any reason to risk snatching defeat from the jaws of victory.

For about a week, that air conditioner sat there - silent; taunting the three of us every day as the cool Spring was increasingly giving way to the humid Summer. During that week, we did learn that it was no mistake that the air conditioner was installed in our room. At least back in the late 70's and early 80's, our Company area (7th Co) was used during the Summer by TANGO Company. TANGO was the holding company for classmates leaving our ranks during Plebe Summer to rejoin the civilian world, and our room was going to be used by the TANGO Company Officer or by someone on his staff.

With that question answered, there remained the final big one. "Can we and/or should we turn it on?" No directive came from our Company Officer or Firsties; and yet everyday, the air conditioner looked at us, seductively calling us to turn it on.

In as long as it took God to create the world, the three of us tried to be good Plebes about the matter; but like all great historical dilemmas, good professional intentions gave way to the call of nature. The topic of whether to use the air conditioner or not rose again to the floor with the Maryland humidity melting away much of our earlier resolve. In the middle of this discussion, Sam suddenly arose from his seat and turned it on. The debate was over. In one simple act, he displayed the boldness of Farragut at Mobile Bay and the inner strength of Mitscher at the Marianas. ("He who will not risk, cannot win" – JPJ)

As the whirling sound and cool air started to fill our room, the three of us sat quietly, motionless, braced for shock awaiting the Brigade "gestapo" to come barging into our room. In a matter of seconds we would find out if we would enjoy a nice cool, comfortable May or be eternally marching in the very same hot, humid air we were trying to escape. One minute passed. Two minutes passed. A half hour passed and not one word from anyone. In fact, no one ever said anything to us about it. Sure, upper classmen would walk by, look at us with a disbelieving expression shaking their heads and say, "Plebes with air conditioners, hmmf" and then walk away, but no one ever said for us to turn it off or not to use it.

Needless to say we enjoyed our new toy like three fat cats, with Sam being the biggest cat of all. "Old Sam" just didn't love sleep but was addicted to it. He would wake up in the morning looking forward to a "nooner" only to wakeup from his nap to begin the countdown to taps.

Having, now, an air conditioner at his disposal was the cat's meow. He just loved turning it on to "Siesta" mode and hitting his coveted rack earning a new title for himself as "Siesta Sam." The air conditioner gave the three of us great notoriety making us very popular amongst classmates and select upper classmen who were allowed to visit and cool off a little.

With the unexpected help of our NAVY air conditioner, we survived our final exams and final chow calls. Maybe, in fact, that air conditioner was a good luck token from Heaven or even Tecumseh himself. Steve (Sam) would remain my roommate for five more semesters, possibly hoping that, with me at his side, lightning would strike again and get another air conditioner for every May. Sam would go on to discover another type of cooling aboard our nuclear "Boomers." John would go on to varsity lacrosse fame and Marine Corps aviation; and I would go on to gain NFO wings of gold and a cameo appearance in "Top Gun." I now live in Las Vegas where it is very hot - so I think I'll go lie down, play some mellow music and turn on the a/c to "Siesta."

Luke Koeller '83

Editor's Note: After graduating in May 1983, Luke earned his NFO wings for the E-2C Hawkeye. He then served consecutive tours with VAW-114, VBQ-33, and USS Kitty Hawk (CV 63). He participated in Operations "Ernest Will," "Restore Hope," and "Southern Watch." Joining the Reserves in 1994, he was promoted to Lieutenant Commander and currently drills with FITCPAC 0194 in San Diego. He lives in Las Vegas, NV, where he is employed by the US Postal Service and is working on his Masters Degree in Management.

Command Performance

The door burst open and in stepped a Company upper classman doing his bit to scare the wits out of unsuspecting Plebes. Such intrusions were part and parcel of the training and indoctrination Plebes came to expect.

"Which one of you two can carry a tune?" he asked. I saw my wife (read roommate) raise a hesitant hand. "OK, both of you come around tonight and you (addressing my wife) be ready to sing *"I'm Always Chasing Rainbows."*

We showed up at the appointed time. The upperclassman and his two wives had us brace up and shout our names. I was pushed against the wall and told to "sit on the green bench" – a murderous exercise in which your back is flat against the wall, knees out and you pretend that you're sitting. Then he turned to my wife and said, "OK, let's have it."

When they heard the first strains of the beautiful Chopin etude-turned-pop song, they were transfixed. My wife had a glorious baritone voice, and he played it for all he was worth. Pretty soon upper-classmen from adjoining rooms came in too and when the song ended, he was told to sing it again. All this time I was getting painful cramps in my thighs and my knees began to oscillate uncontrollably. "Am I the forgotten man?" I uttered. "OK, carry on, but shut up." Welcome words for this miserable Plebe.

Now that he had a standing-room-only audience, my wife really let go for his *encore.* I was sure I saw moist eyes and rapt expressions in the faces of several of the listeners, including my taskmaster.

When my wife reached the end of the lyrics and the words, "…I never even make a gain, believe me…" he motioned to his audience to join him in singing the final phrase. And they did! When it ended there was a moment of silence, followed by tumultuous applause. And the upper-classmen couldn't help themselves, but came forward and shook his hand – "spooning" we called it and it meant that the lucky Plebe was allowed to "carry on" and be treated as an equal. They were so moved by the song and the occasion that they even spooned me.

It was an unforgettable evening for my roommate and me and it showed that upperclass authoritarianism had its limits and could be breached under the right circumstances. Of course, upper-classmen who missed my wife's performance continued to ensure that we had a proper Plebe year.

Anonymous

P.S. Today, many years later, the two "wives" continue to be close friends, but the songster is afraid that if his identity became known there would be no end to requests for "I'm Always Chasing Rainbows."

Name That Tune

Back in the late forties, with World War II but a piece of recent history, Midshipmen were often known to write their own chapters in the annuls of Academy folklore. Luke Capone was then, and still is, a fantastic piano player. He would often sit down and entertain family and friends any time he happened upon an available upright, baby grand or other keyboard configuration.

One time while at the Naval Academy he and his roommate found a small piano in the basement of Bancroft Hall. It looked out of place and, from the accumulation of dust, it was obvious that it had not been used in quite a while. What a waste! With a bit of planning and a lot of effort, they managed to move this unwieldy instrument up to their room without apparent damage and still in tune.

Though short lived, the rest of the Midshipmen in his company thoroughly enjoyed singing along with Luke to melodies from this new-found attraction. It didn't take very long for a duty officer to find the piano during a routine inspection of the area, but he wasn't quite sure how to proceed. He stopped and pondered the situation for a minute of two before deciding to write Luke and his roommate up for "failure to properly stow a musical instrument on top of the locker."

Tom Seelye '49

XXVII

Now these are the Laws of the Navy

And many and mighty are they.

But the hull and the deck and the keel

And the truck of the law is -- OBEY.

hunt '67

The Blue Jacket

Back in the Spring of 1968, after having reported to my first ship, the *USS Warrington* (DD-843) as ASW Officer, we made a five-month overseas deployment to northern Europe, with ports of call in Stockholm, Bergen, Rotterdam and Bremen. I handled my fair share of collateral duties, including mess treasurer, weapons safety officer, athletic event coordinator, and many others, which seemed to fill all available awake time that was not spent on my primary duties. As we prepared to berth in Bremen, one of my collateral assignments to which up until then I had given little attention, suddenly became priority one. This was honor guard officer. Being the flagship for Destroyer Squadron 24, we were to receive a visit from CINCUSNAVEUR.

I assembled the honor guard on the fantail and we practiced a few drills, including port arms, inspection arms, the whole nine yards, and then waited patiently at parade rest for the important arrival. We didn't have to wait long. Right on schedule, we heard the Admiral piped aboard and immediately thereafter he inspected our honor guard, taking the time to exchange a few words with each sailor in the guard. When I gave my final sword salute, Admiral John S. McCain, Jr., told me that he would like to address the troops. He then proceeded to speak for nearly 15 minutes about the importance of the "blue jacket" and what our presence means in Europe and the other nations around the world. It was a moving and motivating message that nearly brought a tear to one's eyes. At the conclusion of his remarks, I gave another sword salute and he was off to the Commodore's cabin for tea.

What was amazing to me was the fact that he spent less than five minutes with the Commodore. Before we knew it he was being piped off the ship. Here we had the senior U.S. Naval Commander in all of Europe spending more time with the honor guard and addressing the enlisted men than he spent with the Commanding Officers of the Ship and Squadron. Boy, was I ever impressed. The lesson I learned was that the bluejacket, the fighting man, is the heart and soul of any military contingent; that they may be asked at any time to put their lives on the line for their country; and that no matter how skillful the leadership, the results will be for naught if you do not have men (and women) who feel their jobs are important and appreciated, regardless of rank.

Richard Zino '67

God Bless the U.S.A.

As a 2/C Midshipman in my first real leadership opportunity, Plebe Summer Detail was both challenging and exciting. The early mornings, long runs, endless push-ups and constant review of Plebe rates at all hours (and in all forms) were grueling but also fostered a strong bond between me, as squad leader, and my squad. We spent so much time together that I knew these eight Plebes probably better than I knew my own roommate.

As the weeks passed and their knowledge and confidence grew steadily, I became extremely proud of their achievements and motivation. The week before Parent's Weekend was a busy time and they were well deserving of the upcoming visit for they too were proud of their achievements.

Just as we were all about to march to T-Court and exhibit noon meal formation to hundreds of proud family members and friends, I wanted to share my pride with them. In our summer whites, the first time any of them had ever worn them, we did our usual motivational push-ups. But, this time there was no counting these push-ups. Instead we went to the beat of Lee Greenwood's "God Bless the USA." I had never seen "my Plebes" so proud and never felt such a great feeling of accomplishment. To this day I still have fond memories of what was the start of a truly memorable weekend.

Tara Caroselli '94

Vice Admiral Rich Mies' Address
at the 30 Year Retirement Ceremony

Admiral Larson, Fellow flag officers, Fellow classmates, Distinguished guests, and most importantly family and friends of the seven Class of 1967 retirees we honor today.

Good afternoon. What a wonderful homecoming. I always enjoy returning to our roots at the Naval Academy, and today is even more special. Like so many graduates of this institution, I am flooded with memories each time I drive through the gates and see the monuments and buildings that have by now become a constant in our lives. The memories remain incredibly vivid, filled with an emotion that never seems to wane.

Today is a very special day and I approach my responsibilities with a great sense of humility and gratitude to recognize our classmates - both those that have gone before us and those whom we honor today.

There is a wonderful symmetry to life. It is full of beginnings and endings, sometimes happy - sometimes sad. But ultimately there is balance - and there is change. The military, perhaps more than any other profession, is comprised of beginnings and endings. Like the alpha and the omega, the first and last letters of the Greek alphabet, beginnings and endings often define what John Masefield called the "vagrant gypsy life" we lead in the military. One task is ending - and another beginning. As one door closes, another opens. And one door will close and another will open for seven of us here today. It is a happy occasion honoring their service rendered, and a sad occasion, for the military will sorely miss them.

Today I have two tasks. The first is to honor the retirement of five Navy Captains, five captains who have run the race and who have finished strong, who "Didn't give up the ship" and who have decided to leave the Naval Service just as they entered it - in Lord Nelson's words,- "as a band of brothers,"- from here where it all began surrounded in this historic hall by so many memories of our great naval traditions..

The second task is also important and concerns all of us in this room; it is to pause and mark a major landmark, to celebrate the service of the United States Naval Academy Class of 1967, to the Navy, and to our nation. For in a very real sense, today marks the curtain call on the main act of the naval service of the Class of '67. Yes there will be a few encores, several of us will continue to play on for a few years, but in the main, today's ceremony will signal the end of an era, the era of the Class of '67. And what an era it has been. It's said "Success is a journey not a destination." And our class has certainly had a great journey. Allow me to reminisce for a few moments with you. John Masefield once wrote:

> "I must go down to the sea again,
> for the call of the running tide
> is a wild call and a clear call
> that may not be denied."

And it was a wild, clear call that brought many of us to the Naval Academy in 1963. On that fateful day in June, 34 years ago, some twelve hundred fifty young men reported to form up the Naval Academy Class of 1967 and, for most of us, our lives were forever changed.

When Rear Admiral Kirkpatrick - Uncle Charlie - a man we came to love and respect, swore us in, he imbued us with the spirit of John Paul Jones - "Sign up young man and sail with me." He told us time and time again "You can do anything you set your minds to do." And many of us set our minds on being just half the officer Rear Admiral Kirkpatrick was.

On that first day our world changed dramatically. We became very focused inside the cloistered confines of the yard and inside the walls of Mother B. All of us have our own memories of that beginning - - that first haircut, learning to march and square corners, the pain of a large atlas if you lost a bet, spit shining shoes.

But the world outside the walls continued on without us. Just before we arrived that June, the nuclear submarine *Thresher* sank in the worst submarine disaster of our time. The Cold War was in full swing, John F. Kennedy had just been elected President, and the Beatles scored their first big success in the United States.

In early August of our Plebe summer a young, new President addressed us. As part of his speech he said: "I want to express the strong hope that all of you who have come to the Academy as Plebes will stay with the Navy. I can think of no more rewarding a career. You will have a chance in the next 10, 20 and 30 years to serve the course of freedom and your country all over the globe, to hold positions of the highest responsibility, to recognize that upon your good judgment in many cases may well rest not only the well being of the men with whom you serve, but also in a very real sense the security of your country. I can imagine a no more rewarding career. Any man who may be asked in this century what he did to make his life worth while, I think can respond with a good deal of pride and satisfaction: I served in the U.S. Navy". Those were prophetic words - the men before you are their living proof.

At the end of his speech President Kennedy granted amnesty "to whoever needs it, whoever deserves it." I don't know if we deserved it, but I know plenty of us needed it.

Several months later, President Kennedy was assassinated and I think most of us remember exactly where we were on that November afternoon when the word was passed.

During the next four years we mastered - or at least survived challenging courses fondly nicknamed "steam" and "wires" and "skinny." We learned important lessons - not just in the formal classrooms, but in the informal classrooms of the parade grounds, the athletic fields, the mess tables, and in the halls of Mother B. Lessons that would carry us through life. And we learned the concept of honor and the meaning of class ties that would bind us forever.

Most of us were too young or too busy to fully appreciate the meaning of the Naval Academy's motto - *Ex Scientia Tridens* - From Knowledge Seapower - but those early struggles became tomorrow's strengths.

Over the next four years we also saw America become involved in the war in Vietnam, and many of our upperclassmen to become prisoners of war or casualties in that conflict. There were many other dramatic changes in the world beyond Bancroft Hall - a world from which we were often isolated.

- The civil rights movement
- The introduction of the Ford Mustang
- The opening of the Capital Beltway
- The beginning of Master Card
- The first episode of Star Trek
- The first Super Bowl

In June of 1967, "6/7/67" to be exact and no mere coincidence I might state, 890 of our class graduated. 770 were sworn in as Ensigns, 85 as 2nd Lieutenants in the

Marine Corps, 2 were commissioned in the Air Force and 10 were commissioned in the Army. Four classmates had tragically lost their lives along the way - one sadly on graduation day. Lyndon Johnson was President, Admiral David MacDonald was the Chief of Naval Operations, and Rear Admiral Draper Kauffman was the Superintendent. When Vice President Hubert Humphrey presented our diplomas we couldn't wait to leave. In fact, our class song was - I'm sure you will all remember as we sang it at most of our class functions - "We gotta get out of this place." Now 30 years later, we frequently can't wait to come back.

As new Ensigns and Second Lieutenants, we began our service to our country. Young, headstrong, and energetic, we left to make our mark on the Fleet and to serve our nation. We scattered to assignments around the globe.

The rock solid four-year experience at the Naval Academy prepared us well for the challenges that lay ahead and would be with us forever. Four years of setting goals, weighing values, and maturing into leaders.

Who indeed could have predicted all that would happen in the journey of the next 30 years? Who could have comprehended that time would pass so fast? We started our naval service in a time of tremendous upheaval and change in America and the world. We were at war in Vietnam. Many of our classmates served there, and three of today's honorees went in-country. Eight of our classmates made the supreme sacrifice in that faraway conflict, and one was a prisoner of war.

Then came the post-Vietnam drawdown. We experienced some tough times. Some of our best people left in droves, we had racial problems, we became a hollow force, our ships could not get underway. Our service and our sacrifice became unpopular. We endured a period of broken promises and unrealized hopes. But we stuck it out, we held our course, focused and determined. Indeed some of our classmates departed the pattern. But in the end we steadied up on course, went back to the basics of our vocation and took up the clarion call of pride and professionalism.

In the second half of our class journey, we soared. The Maritime Strategy provided us a strategic vision. We transitioned to an all-volunteer force. We invested in new technology but more importantly, we invested in people and pride and discipline. And in 1989 in magnificent irony, the Berlin wall fell and the *Evil Empire* collapsed. We won the Cold War without ever firing a shot. And in the frenzied finale of our journey, we fought a desert war of immense success and popularity and finally received the tribute for which we had waited so long.

Of course, there have been many individual milestones along the way. The day we married, the births of our children, the loss of a loved one. But there have also been many shared ones - the class reunions, the promotions, the shared sorrow of the loss of our classmates such as Mike Smith on *Challenger*, the infamous *Slummer* get-togethers, the shared deployments, separations, and sacrifices, the shared accomplishments.

So what's the point? As we look back on our 34 years as a class, what counts? We have commanded ships and squadrons and battalions of all sorts. We have won medals and awards. We have flown in space and stood at both the North and South Poles. We have fought in deserts and jungles and over, and on, and under the oceans of the world. We have provided a strong presence which ensured peace and eventually won a war that many people thought couldn't be won or wasn't worth the price.

We have served our Navy and our Nation proudly. The plaques and certificates that hang on our "I love me walls" (at least those that our wives didn't make us unload in the last yard sale) attest to achievements of a tangible sort. But in my mind, when we look back on our service and its true meaning, it's the cause we served and the people we encountered along the way that count. Many we can't remember or maybe never really knew. It's been a long journey and it hasn't been easy. The statistics are a stark reminder. Twelve hundred fifty entered the Class of '67, eight hundred ninety graduated, and fifty are no longer with us.

And so it has come full circle back to where this class was first born. We left with enthusiasm and hope, we toiled through a period of confusion and rejection, we triumphed in a spectacular blaze of glory and now we return for a moment of reflection. JFK was right after all. There is no more rewarding career. Charlie Kirkpatrick and Draper Kauffman would have been very proud of our class. I know RADM Charlie Minter, our second Superintendent who is here today, is very proud of this class. We served well. We leave the Navy better because of our service.

Today marks an ending of sorts for our class and especially the retirees before you but it also marks a new beginning. We begin a new journey as we pass on the watch. Whether to pursue second careers, to work an improving our golf handicap or to spend time with our grandchildren.

Take a look in front of you. Great people like these are responsible for the successes of the last three decades. Their biographies are in the program, and if I have one frustration today it is that we can't honor each of them adequately. These are people who were more interested in outcomes rather than incomes. Who thought more of their country than themselves.

Each one of them is a great story:
- of responsibilities sought and well discharged
- of opportunities seized
- of uncertainties faced and overcome
- of caring leadership competence, and character.
Let me give you a little flavor of their stories...

Captain Dick Field, hailing from Arlington Texas - a nuclear submariner and a former shipmate who served challenging tours on the Pacific Fleet and a submarine squadron staff command of the nuclear attack submarine *Pollack*; Commanding Officer of a submarine squadron in Charleston; Executive Director of the Strategic Advisory Group at US Strategic Command; Two masters degrees and a graduate of the Naval War College; and a final tour as Professor of Naval Science at Duke, The University of North Carolina and North Carolina State - training our reliefs. Dick's son is a Lieutenant in the U.S. Navy - beginnings and endings. Thanks, Dick.

Captain Tom Kent, another nuclear submariner, a native of Ithaca, New York who followed his brother to the Naval Academy. Tom taught navigation and sailing at the Naval Academy. He worked for Admiral Rickover at Naval Reactors and served with distinction on the staffs of Submarine Squadron Seven, SUBPAC, and both the Atlantic and Pacific Fleets. Tom Commanded the nuclear attack submarines *Tautog* and *Hunley*, the submarine tender. He completed numerous challenging and sensitive operations while in command; and most recently he completed duty as Inspector General of the Atlantic Fleet. Thanks, Tom.

Our third submariner, Captain George Lear, hails from Fresno, California. George served a significant portion of his career at sea on board our ballistic missile submarines; he earned the prestigious gold SSBN patrol pin with 21 strategic deterrent patrols -that's more than four years under water; A senior Instructor at the Purdue University NROTC unit where he earned a Masters degree; Commanding Officer of the nuclear ballistic missile submarine *USS Mariano G. Vallejo* (SSBN 658) and the Trident SSBN *USS Alae* (SSBN 732). Commanded two shore commands instrumental in training our people - Naval Submarine School and most recently as Professor Naval Science at George Washington University NROTC Unit. Thanks, George.

Captain Dick Scott, from Baltimore; a helicopter pilot, Dick earned his wings logging over 4,000 flight hours in more than thirty types of aircraft and has deployed in four different battle groups during his career; he flew over 550 combat missions in support of our Forces in Vietnam; Commanded Helo Squadron 5 on USS *Eisenhower*; served ashore in a full range of assignments ranging from flight instructor in Pensacola, to the Bureau of Naval Personnel, to Naval Air Systems Command earning a masters degree along the way; most recently he served as Assistant Chief of Naval Research. Dick's son is also a Lieutenant in the Navy - another beginning. Thanks, Dick.

And finally, our second naval aviator Captain Bill Vivian, from Grand Haven, Michigan. A talented helicopter pilot, Bill accumulated over 4,700 hours in Naval aircraft. A political military specialist, with two Masters degrees, Bill has spent much of his career working on long range strategy and policy issues in the Philippines and for the Supreme

Allied Commander Europe. He commanded Helicopter Squadron 2 in San Diego aboard the *Kitty Hawk* where he received numerous awards for excellence; Commanded one of our most challenging shore commands, Naval Support Activity, Naples during the recent conflict in former Yugoslavia. Most recently Bill served as Professor of Naval Science at the University of Florida. Thanks, Bill

Now that does not begin to do them justice, but you get the idea. Five classmates, five captains who will leave a legacy of service, dedication, professionalism, perseverance and courage. Thousands and thousands of people are better sailors and better people because of them. How do you recognize the sacrifice and service of a lifetime? That sacrifice, that service is not taken lightly, but neither is it rewarded handsomely. John F. Kennedy once said "Naval officers are paid like bus boys, worked like field hands and then released like old slow halfbacks." A few plaques, pieces of paper, pieces of brightly colored ribbons pinned to their uniforms...all testimony to the appreciation of a nation...at peace, free and prosperous because men like these are willing to serve and sacrifice. They symbolize what the Class of 1967 brought to the Navy. They answered "a wild and clear call" and to paraphrase John Masefield:

> "All they ask is a merry yarn
> from a laughing fellow rover.
> And quiet sleep and a sweet dream
> now that the long trick's over."

Now before I finish I want to thank a very special group of people - our wives and family members who served all of these years beside us. We cannot begin to repay them for their sacrifice - for their service - for their support. For a journey full of separations and constant moves, for our "vagrant gypsy lives" as I mentioned earlier, they stuck by us. They truly are the real heroes of the Navy.

God bless each of you and your families as you get underway for one last duty assignment, independent duty. Enjoy it – you've earned it. Thank you for your sacrifices.

Thank you for letting us share in this special day. God bless the Class of 1967, God bless this institution that nurtured us, God bless the United States Navy, God bless America.

Richard Mies '67

Editor's note: Admiral Richard W. Mies is Commander in Chief, United States Strategic Command, Offutt Air Force Base, Nebraska, with responsibility for all Air Force and Navy strategic nuclear forces supporting the national security objective or strategic deterrence. Admiral Mies served on USS Sunfish (SSN 649) and USS L.Mendel Rivers (SSN 686) and USS Nathan Hale (SSBN 623) before commanding the nuclear attack submarine USS Sea Devil (SSN 664). His command positions include Submarine Development Squadron Twelve; Submarine Group Eight; Allied Submarines, Mediterranean; Submarine Force, U.S.Atlantic Fleet, and Submarine Allied Command, Atlantic. Admiral Mies is married to the former Sheila McCann of Chicago, Illinois. They have two daughters, Rachel Anne and Sara Elizabeth.

Note: Two other members of the class of '67 were also honored in the same retirement ceremony. Their careers were highlighted in an address given by Lieutenant General Mike Williams, USMC, which followed Admiral Mies' presentation.

Glossary

Anchor man	*The Midshipman that graduates last in his class*
Baby	*The jar of mustard on tables in the Mess Hall*
Bilge (to)	*To fail an academic course or courses*
Boat School	*The USNA in Mid vernacular*
B.O.O.W.	*Battalion Officer Of the Watch*
Bracing Up	*Standing at attention, gut sucked in, shoulders back, with chin pulled against the throat, with one's "eyes in the boat"*
Brick	*An unattractive (usually "blind") date*
Bucket	*A low standing, academically*
Bulkhead	*A verticle wall or partition on a ship; also used as a derogatory term for a Midshipman who can't quite grasp a new concept*
Bull	*USNA course in English, History & U.S. Government*
Burble	*To expel column of air vertically from pursed lips upon which, if done properly, a pea can float in mid air*
Bush	*A periodic listing of academic under-performers*
Canoe U.	*Also the USNA in Mid vernacular (see Boat school)*
Carry On	*When a Plebe is allowed to go about his business; relax; stand down; the opposite of bracing up or standing at attention*
Chit	*A note or a small printed form*
CIS chit	*A "dear John" letter (CIS = Christ, I'm sorry)*
Clamp On	*Positioning one's self in a sitting position without the benefit of a chair or the floor; this is done by using one's elbows and knees as the jaws of a vice grip fastened to the edge of a dining hall table; it makes eating rather difficult*

Crab Town	*An affectionate term for the city of Annapolis*
Crab	*An inhabitant of Crab Town, usually a female*
Drag	*A Midshipman's date (also used as a verb)*
Drag House	*A bed and breakfast establishment in Annapolis, sans breakfast, that caters to the dates of Midshipmen*
Dago	*Any foreign language*
Eyes in the boat	*An order to a Plebe to look straight ahead*
Firstie	*First Classman*
Flying Squadron	*The multitude of Midshipmen high-tailing it back from town, usually from a drag house, attempting to return to Bancroft Hall before expiration of liberty, which for Plebes was 2300 hours, for Youngsters 2330 and for second classmen midnight*
Form-2	*A Mid's official notification that he is being put on report*
Fried (getting)	*Being put on report for a conduct infraction*
Gedunk	*Soda fountain or a soda fountain serving; Junk food*
Gouge	*A study aid; an academic reference*
I.C.O.R.	*In Charge Of Room; the roommate responsible for the cleanliness and orderliness on the room; this duty is usually rotated weekly*
I.P.D.	*Improper performance of duty*
Jimmy legs	*The uniformed Yard security police*
Juice	*A science course, such as chemistry, physics, electronics, etc.*
Ladder	*Staircase*

M.O.O.W.	*Midshipman Officer Of the Watch*
N.A.P.S.	*Naval Academy Preparatory School*
Navy Junior	*A son or daughter of a Navy officer*
O and O	*One's sweetheart (a One-and-Only)*
P.D.A.	*Public Display of Affection; this is a punishable offense*
Piece	*The personal armament used during rifle drills and carried in P-Rades*
Plebes	*Freshmen or fourth class Midshipmen*
Podunk	*A small town; where a Mid hails from*
Poontang	*The sexual favors of a drag; as in getting a little*
P-Work	*An all-hands practical work in an academic subject*
P-Rade	*Parade of the Brigade of Midshipmen on Worden Field*
Radiator Squad	*Mids shirking sports participation*
Rate	*What Plebes are given permission to do*
Rates	*The naval trivia, statistics, folklore, and other day-to-day information that Plebes are required to commit to memory and verbalize on command*
Sail-ho	*Calling attention to the presence of an officer*
Sea lawyer	*A master at making excuses*
Second Class	*Midshipmen in third or junior year*
Shoving Out	*Positioning one's self in a sitting position without the aide of a chair; also referred to as "sitting on infinity"*
Skinny	*Accurate information; the answers to a quiz; the "gouge"; also a nickname for some USNA science courses*
Skivvies	*A Mid's underwear*
Slip Stick	*Slide rule calculator (no longer in use)*

Spoon	*When an upperclassman shakes a Plebe's hand; an act of unrestricted friendship bestowed on the Plebe*
Square Corner	*Plebes' compulsory 90-degree turns when negotiating comers in Bancroft hallways*
Square Meal	*Plebes eating by lifting fork- or spoon-fulls of food vertically to mouth height then guiding food horizontally into mouth*
Steam	*Academic subjects including fluid mechanics, propulsion systems, and equipment, mechanical drawing, etc.*
Sub Squad	*The group of Midshipmen who did not complete the mile run in the time allotted and who work on improving their speed in lieu participating in mandatory sports*
Tecumesh	*Figurehead of the USS Delaware, a replica of which stands at the Bancroft Hall end of Stribling Walk; the God of the passing grade*
T-Court	*Tecumseh Court; the area in front of Bancroft Hall where Midshipmen of many companies assemble for inspections and formations*
Tree	*Periodic listing of Mids failing an academic course or courses*
Twins	*Salt and Pepper; as in please pass the...*
Wife	*A Mid's roommate (no longer in use since going coed)*
Wires	*Electrical Engineering*
W.T.Door	*Water Tight Door aboard surface ships; also the name of the mythical Midshipman whose room in Bancroft Hall is always on display*
Yard Bird	*The daughter of an officer assigned to the academic or administrative departments at the USNA*
Youngster	*A sophomore or third class Midshipman*
Y.P.	*Yard Patrol craft used for teaching practical ship handling, navigation and seamanship*

Afterthought

So, you've come to the end of our collection of Annapolis reminiscences. We had to end the book somewhere. And we are sorry if the end came too abruptly and too quickly. But, if you've enjoyed what you've read, take heart. This need not be the end. For there are hundreds -- perhaps thousands -- of stories still untold. If you, dear reader, are an Academy grad, think back to events you can't forget, events that were important to you as a Midshipman, character-building events, amusing events, uplifting events and discouraging events. Put them on paper, or risk their loss forever. And that would be a shame. So, send them along. Please.

There are, without doubt, memorable events happening at the Naval Academy at this very moment, and perhaps the Mids involved will jot down the details. And if, at some point, this book inspires them to contribute their stories to Tales From Annapolis, Volume II or III, etc., they -- and YOU -- will be sharing something very personal and precious with classmates, shipmates, fellow grads, family and friends and any reader who wants to look to the human side behind all the spit and polish.

If you have a story to share, please contact Rich Zino

249 Hamilton Road
Rockville Centre, New York 11570
rzino@aol.com
fax: (516) 764-9509
voice mail: (516) 764-9192

The Authors

Sixty-one graduates of the U.S. Naval Academy submitted stories and anecdotes for this anthology. Some of our contributing authors have included short bios that are printed after their pieces. Most of our contributors just listed their class year, that being reason enough for inclusion in this literary effort. All of them wanted to share memorable experiences of their days in Bancroft Hall. We hope the retelling of these tales of yore will prompt other grads to share their own recollections with shipmates far and wide.

The Editors

Following graduation in 1967, Rich Zino served as ASW Officer and Weapons Department Head on destroyers out of Newport, R.I. He left the Navy in the early seventies and entered the field of telecommunications working for Xerox Corp., International Creative Management and BlackRock. He is active in the Naval Academy Alumni organization and served as president of the New York Chapter from 1993 through 1995. Rich plays clarinet with a popular traditional jazz group, the *Park Avenue Ragtime Jazz and Blues Society*. He enjoys tennis, bicycling, swimming, writing, and during the summer months is a card-carrying beach bum.

Paul Laric graduated with the Class of 1949, served on the aircraft carrier *Coral Sea*, on staff duty with *CINCNELM*, Naples, Italy, and aboard *Neches AO-47*. He then embarked on a career in Public Relations with New York – based corporations and agencies, winding up with his own consultancy before retirement. He was president of the Naval Academy Association of New York and served as trustee of the USNA Alumni Association. Among his published works are books, *Fractured Italian* and *Maribor Remembered*, and articles in business, sports and consumer publications. The Larics divide their time between a New York apartment and a cottage in the Berkshires, which they share with their dog and – at last count – three cats.